WORLD WAR II
FROM ORIGINAL SOURCES

THE
SPITFIRE

EDITED BY BOB CARRUTHERS

Pen & Sword
AVIATION

This edition published in 2013 by
Pen & Sword Aviation
An imprint of
Pen & Sword Books Ltd
47 Church Street
Barnsley
South Yorkshire
S70 2AS

First published in Great Britain in 2012 in digital format by
Coda Books Ltd.

ISBN 978 1 78159 114 7

A CIP catalogue record for this book is
available from the British Library

Printed and bound by
CPI Group (UK) Ltd, Croydon, CR0 4YY

Pen & Sword Books Ltd incorporates the Imprints of Pen & Sword Aviation, Pen &
Sword Family History, Pen & Sword Maritime, Pen & Sword Military, Pen & Sword
Discovery, Pen & Sword Politics, Pen & Sword Atlas, Pen & Sword Archaeology,
Wharncliffe Local History, Wharncliffe True Crime, Wharncliffe Transport, Pen
& Sword Select, Pen & Sword Military Classics, Leo Cooper, The Praetorian Press,
Claymore Press, Remember When, Seaforth Publishing and Frontline Publishing

For a complete list of Pen & Sword titles please contact
PEN & SWORD BOOKS LIMITED
47 Church Street, Barnsley, South Yorkshire, S70 2AS, England
E-mail: enquiries@pen-and-sword.co.uk
Website: www.pen-and-sword.co.uk

CONTENTS

- C H A P T E R   1 -

SPITFIRE: THE LEGEND

PROBABLY ONE of the most famous fighter planes of all time, the Spitfire became by the latter stages of World War Two a superb fighter aircraft. Contrary to popular belief the Spitfire was not the main aircraft in the battle of Britain - that honour goes to the Hurricane, but it did serve in every theatre of war including the naval version, the Seafire.

According to Air Commodore Alan Deere, "There can be no doubt that victory in the Battle of Britain was made possible by the Spitfire. Although there were more Hurricanes than Spitfires in the battle, the Spitfire was the RAF's primary weapon because of its better all-round capability. The Hurricane alone could not have won this great air battle, but the Spitfire (if in sufficient numbers) could have done so."

Lieutenant Colonel William R. Dunn, USAAF ex-no 71 (Eagle) Squadron, Royal Air Force, adds, "The Spitfire was a thing of beauty to behold, in the air or on the ground, with the graceful lines of its slim fuselage, its elliptical wing and tailplane. It looked like a fighter, and it certainly proved to be just that in the fullest meaning of the term. It was an aircraft with a personality all of its own - docile at times, swift and deadly at others - a fighting machine 'par excellence'.

One must really have known the Spitfire in flight to fully understand and appreciate its thoroughbred flying characteristics. It was the finest and, in its days of glory, provided the answer to the fighter pilot's dream - a perfect combination of all the good qualities required in a truly outstanding fighter aircraft.

Once you've flown a Spitfire, it spoils you for all other fighters. Every other aircraft seems imperfect in one way or another."

P/O H.G.Niven, 601 & 602 Squadrons says, "Flying the Spitfire was like driving a sports car. It was faster than the old Hurricane much more delicate. You couldn't roll it very fast, but you could make it go up and down much easier. A perfect lady. It wouldn't do anything wrong.

The Hurricane would drop a wing if you stalled it coming in, but a Spitfire would come wafting down. You couldn't snap it into a spin. Beautiful to fly, although very stiff on the ailerons - you had to jam your elbow against the side to get the leverage to move them. And so fast!!! If you shut the throttle in a Hurricane you'd come to a grinding halt; in a Spitfire you just go whistling on."

INVASION PENDING!

By June 1940, Continental Western Europe languished under Hitler, as Britain's newly appointed wartime Prime Minister Winston Churchill shrugged off the shadow of the First World War's failed Dardanelles Campaign, to lead his people in stubborn, arrogant and seemingly futile resistance against the odds.

Churchill said, "What General Weygand called the Battle of France is over. I expect that the Battle of Britain is about to begin. Upon this battle depends the survival of Christian civilization.

… The whole fury and might of the enemy must very soon be turned on us. Hitler knows that he will have to break us in this Island or lose the war.

… Let us therefore brace ourselves to our duties, and so bear ourselves that, if the British Empire and its Commonwealth last for a thousand years, men will still say, 'This was their finest hour.'"

Hitler readied 160,000 assault troops, Rhine barges, and supporting forces for the invasion of England, codenamed Operation Sealion. For the invasion to succeed, *Luftwaffe* air supremacy over the landing zones was vital. The RAF was to be either destroyed or pushed back from its coastal bases in Southern England so that the landings could take place. This preliminary operation was to be achieved under the codename Operation Eagle.

The British could muster scarcely 3 fully armed divisions in defence of their Isle after the losses in France, so Home Guard units of local defence volunteers aged 17 to 65 were raised - initially armed with pitchforks, shotguns and a handful of rounds each - and were expected to defend against well armed & experienced German shocktroops.

The RAF had also been seriously mauled supporting the allied armies on the continent, leaving barely 300 front-line interceptors to defend the kingdom. What aircraft remained was due to the foresight of Air Chief Marshal Sir Hugh Dowding refusing to send any more squadrons to France.

The stakes were high - America had yet to enter the war, and if Britain fell, Hitler's secret ambition to conquer Russia would likely succeed. The fate of the world hung in the hands of the young allied pilots. It was said in America that Britain would last no more than 6 weeks before capitulating.

Spitfires of No. 611 RAuxAF Squadron photographed in Digby, Autumn 1939. Dowding's decision of not deploying the Spitfires into France was based on supply rather than tactical considerations. The production rate for the Spitfire was too slow to support the rapid attrition rate inevitable with overseas deployment. Spitfires entered combat in May 1940 over Dunkirk.

OPERATION EAGLE - THE BATTLE OF BRITAIN

Fighter Command pilots flying Spitfire Mk.I's and Hawker Hurricane's (the RAF's other front-line service fighter) found themselves pitted against the cream of Hitler's undefeated *Luftwaffe* veterans, in a desperate and almost hopeless attempt to maintain air superiority over their vital forward airfields and radar stations.

On September 15, during the height of the air battle, Winston Churchill asked his famous question "What other reserves have we?" to which Air Vice-Marshal Park answered "We have none" - Fighter Command had committed all its reserves to the air battle that day, but the vastly outnumbered Fighter Command pilots gave no quarter, and the tide began to turn.

By Autumn 1940 the massed daylight strikes against Britain's front line defences had eased - Hitler had been rebuffed for the first time, but a strategic terror campaign known as The Blitz soon followed. Nightly massed aerial bombing of English population centres was hoped to weaken civilian resolve and topple the wartime government, but Hitler had already postponed the invasion of England until 1941 and re-focused his attention on the upcoming invasion of Russia.

The massed aerial battles fought in the skies over the English countryside by The Few in the summer of 1940 had saved Britain from invasion in her Darkest Hour and ultimately turned the tide of the Second World War in Europe. The graceful but deadly Spitfire became the symbol of that most important of allied victories. As Winston Churchill famously out it, "Never in the field of human conflict was so much owed by so many to so few."

Designed by trophy-winning aircraft designer Reginald J. Mitchell and manufactured by Vickers-Armstrong's' subsidiary Supermarine, Spitfire fighters were made to be fast and manoeuvrable. The first prototype, K5054, took flight on 5 Mar 1936 at Eastleigh Aerodrome, Hampshire, England, United

Kingdom; this first flight did not live up to Mitchell's expectations, but Mitchell knew that he had a good foundation to work with. After much hard work, it was finally accepted by the British Air Ministry; upon that time, director of Vickers-Armstrong's Sir Robert MacLean named it Spitfire, which was his daughter's nickname. The first order was placed on 3 June 1936 for 310 units, and it took two years for Supermarine to prepare for full-scale production thanks to the complex design. The wings, for example, were thin, covered with stressed metal skin, and of a revolutionary elliptical shape. Notably, it was reported that a German Bf 109 fighter took a third less time to build than a Spitfire aircraft. However, Supermarine was still able to produce them in great numbers. During the design's production life, 20,351 were built, including the Seafire carrier fighter variant, two-seater trainer variant, and many others. The design was produced in greater numbers than any other Allied fighter design, and was the only Allied fighter in production at the outbreak of the European War that was still in production at its end.

The first Spitfire aircraft to enter service with the No. 19 Squadron RAF arrived at Duxford, England, Britain on 4 August 1938; unfortunately, Mitchell did not live to see this event. Men of the No. 19 Squadron RAF reported that the fighter had leakage and engine starting problems, but overall the performance was outstanding. By September 1939, when the European War began, 400 Spitfire aircraft were in service with the RAF, and a further 2,000 were on order. The first Spitfire fighters lost were to a friendly fire incident on 6 September over Medway, England. Together with the venerable Hawker Hurricane fighters, these two types of fighters defended Britain from Germany's aerial invasion during the Battle of Britain; while the slower Hurricane fighters often acted as bomber interceptors, the speedy and manoeuvrable Spitfire fighters targeted their escorting fighters. Their speed was not only an effective offensive weapon in attacking enemy fighters, but the speed was also a reason for many Spitfire pilots' survival as well, particularly when given chase by enemy fighters; author Stephen Bungay noted that "not until the advent of the first swept-wing jets in 1949 was there anything which could catch it".

Most Spitfire fighters had their fuel tanks lined with Linatex to prevent leakage through bullet holes, which prevented fire during combat. This lining was proven to be very effective, thus it was later applied to fuel tanks for Hurricane fighters as well.

In late 1941, with the introduction of the Fw 190 fighters on the German side, Spitfire losses climbed until upgraded versions reached adequate numbers. To counter this disadvantage, some Spitfire Mk XII and Mk XIV were equipped with the new and more powerful Rolls-Royce Griffon engines, making them much more capable in low-level combat situations. The first of the Griffon-powered Spitfire fighters took flight on 27 Nov 1941, and the pilots of these new variants found themselves wielding effective weapons. Pilots such as Flight Officer Ken Collier reported that their Griffon-powered Spitfire fighters were so fast and agile that they were capable of flying in parallel with German V1 rockets and then close in to tip the rockets' wings to cause them to crash. The Griffon-powered Spitfire fighters were so lethal that German *Luftwaffe* General Adolf Galland noted "the best thing about the Spitfire Mk XIV was that there were so few of them".

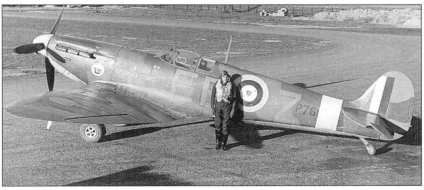

Squadron Leader D.O. Finlay, the Commanding Officer of No. 41 Squadron RAF and former British Olympic hurdler, standing by his Supermarine Spitfire Mark IIA (P7666, EB-Z) Observer Corps, at Hornchurch, Essex.

Beginning in Mar 1942, many of the Spitfire fighters flew off of carrier decks to be transferred to Malta to aid the defence there. In 1943, as Allied bombing missions increased in range, Spitfire fighters with their shorter ranges were limited to bomber escort missions to northwestern France only, while bombing missions into Germany were escorted by American fighters that had longer range. After the Normandy invasion, Spitfire squadrons were moved to France to operate from tactical airfields close to German lines. As the German *Luftwaffe* weakened toward the end of the war, they began providing tactical ground support for the advancing army units.

Operations off Norway and in the Mediterranean Sea revealed that the British Royal Navy did not possess carrier fighters that were capable enough to deal with modern fighters. Given that the RAF had already successfully used Spitfire and Hurricane fighters, the Admiralty demanded to test them as carrier fighters. "Sea Hurricane" fighters were modified from Hurricane fighters; they were considered the less favourable of the two. "Sea Spitfire" fighters, on the other hand, seemed to be ideal. The first carrier landing of modified Spitfire fighters for carrier operations was Lieutenant Commander H.P. Bramwell, commanding officer of the Royal Navy Fighter School. In the River Clyde in Scotland, United Kingdom, he successfully landed a modified Spitfire fighter on the carrier HMS Illustrious, which was anchored in the river; this took place on 10 Jan 1942. After further successful landings by Bramwell, 250 Spitfire Mk VB and VC aircraft were slated to be converted for carrier use. These new conversions became the first of Seafire fighters. Seafire IIC variants were the first purpose-built carrier fighters of the Royal Navy Fleet Air Arm. Later in the war, folding wings were introduced. United States Navy pilot Corky Meyer made a positive comment about the Seafire fighter he test flew during the Joint USAAF/US Navy Fighter Conference in Florida, United States in Mar 1943:

Without argument, the Spitfire/Seafire configuration was

probably the most beautiful fighter ever to emerge from a drawing board. Its elliptical wing and long, slim fuselage were visually most delightful, and its flight characteristics equaled its aerodynamic beauty.

The Seafire had such delightful upright flying qualities that knowing it had an inverted fuel and oil system, I decided to try inverted "figure-8s". They were as easy as pie, even when hanging by the complicated, but comfortable, British pilot restraint harness. I was surprised to hear myself laughing as if I were crazy. I have never enjoyed a flight in attitude. It was clear to see how few exhausted, hastily trained, Battle of Britain pilots were able to fight off Hitler's hordes for so long, and so successfully, with it.

The Lend-Lease Royal Navy Wildcats, Hellcats and Corsair fighters were only workhorses. The Seafire III was a dashing stallion!

During the Pacific War, Seafire fighters were operated from British carriers and played a vital role in Task Force 57's mission to protect the southern flank during the Okinawa campaign. Their main tasks were typically defensive in nature due to their medium to low altitude performance, making them ideal weapons to guard against the diving kamikaze special attack aircraft that were used by the Japanese by this stage of the war. British Royal Navy Fleet Air Arm pilot Lieutenant Commander Mike Crosley of 880 Naval Air Squadron aboard HMS Implacable commented that "we felt that the Seafire, of all aircraft, would be the best possible defence in such circumstances, and we were not too frightened provided we could see the kamikazes coming." Nevertheless, due to the speed that kamikaze aircraft dove in, even the Seafire fighters could only shoot down some of the many suicide aircraft diving at British carriers. During the Okinawa campaign, British carriers were hit 7 times by special attack aircraft.

After the war, Spitfire aircraft were used in many air forces around the world, including Sweden, Italy, Israel, and many

Spitfires take to the sky over Britain 1941.

others. Some of them remained in service well into the 1960s. In the post-war age of jet fighters, many pilots remain attached to the Spitfire design. George Unwin, who flew with No. 19 Squadron RAF during the Battle of Britain, recalled:

It was a super aircraft, it was absolutely. It was so sensitive on the controls. There was no heaving, or pulling and pushing and kicking. You just breathed on it and when you wanted, if you wanted to turn, you just moved your hands slowly and she went... She really was the perfect flying machine. I've never flown anything sweeter. I've flown jets right up to the Venom, but nothing, nothing like her. Nothing like a Spitfire.

SPITFIRE TIMELINE

- **1st December 1934:** British Air Ministry issued a contract to Supermarine for monoplane fighters powered by the Rolls Royce PV 12 Merlin engines; later to be named Spitfire.

- **5th March 1936:** Supermarine prototype 200 aircraft took flight from Eastleigh airfield in England, United Kingdom; this aircraft was to become the Spitfire.

- **3rd June 1936:** The British Air Ministry placed an order for 310 Spitfire fighters at £4500 each.

- **27th June 1936:** First public appearance of the Spitfire prototype at Royal Air Force Pageant, Hendon.

- **11th June 1937:** R.J. Mitchell dies of cancer aged 42.

- **14th May 1938:** First production Spitfire (K9787) flies for first time.

- **4th August 1938:** The first Spitfire fighter deployed into service went to No.19 Squadron RAF The squadron reported good performance, but the fighter had leaks in the engine and was difficult to start.

- **3rd September 1939:** Outbreak of the World War II. The RAF has eight fully equipped Spitfire squadrons, with 187 Spitfires.

- **24th September 1939:** First flight of the Mk II.

- **August 1940:** No. 611 squadron at Digby becomes the first squadron to receive the Mk II.

- **January 1941:** First Mk V produced.

- **February 1941:** No.92 squadron the first to receive the Mk V.

- **March 1941:** Decision taken to mass-produce the Mk V instead of the Mk III.

- **September 1941:** First flight of the prototype Mk III with the Merlin 61 engine as used in the Mk IX, VII and VII.

- **October 1941:** Appearance of the Mk Vc with the universal "c" wing.

- **December 1941:** First production Mk VIs completed.

- **10th January 1942:** Lieutenant Commander H.P. Bramwell made the first landing of a modified Spitfire fighter abroad carrier Illustrious in the River Clyde, Scotland. The success led to the development of the carrier version of the Spitfire design, Seafire.

- **21st February 1942:** First prototype Mk IX takes to the air.

- **7th March 1942:** First overseas deployment of the Spitfire when fifteen Mk Vbs are flown to Malta from HMS Eagle.

- **April 1942:** Mk IX assessed by AFDU.

- **June 1942:** Mk IX enters full production.

- **July 1942:** First Mk IXs enter operational service.

- **August 1942:** First production Mk VII completed.

- **12th September 1942:** Mk IX takes part in highest combat of the war, at 43,000 feet over Southampton against a Ju 86R, which escapes.

- **October 1942:** End of Mk VI production.

- **November 1942:** First Mk VIIIs produced.

- **8th November 1942:** The first combat victory by the new Seafire Naval fighter occurred when a New Zealander, Sub-Lieutenant A.S. Long, shot down a Vichy French Martin 167 bomber over Mers-el-kebir harbour in French Algeria.

- **27th November 1942:** The British Seafire F III carrier fighter reached the 894 Naval Air Squadron.

- **February 1943:** First Griffon powered Mk XIIs enter service with No.41 squadron.

- **June 1943:** Mk VIII enters service with No. 145 Squadron on Malta.

- **January 1944:** Mk XIV entered front line service with No.610 squadron.

- **Early 1944:** End of Mk VII production.

- **April 1944:** Mk VIIIs reach Australia, replaced Mk Vc around Darwin.

- **5th October 1944:** Mk IXbs of 401 squadron become first allied aircraft to shoot down an Me 262.

- **1st April 1945:** British Sub Lieutenant R.H. Reynolds's Seafire carrier shot down two A6M5 Zero fighters: these were the first Seafire victories against Zero Fighters. Mk 21 goes operational with No.91 Squadron.

- **15th August 1945:** VJ Day was declared in Britain.

The Mk.V was introduced in 1941 as an interim version of the aircraft to counter the threat from the new German Bf.109F that was entering service with the *Luftwaffe*. The major change from the Mk.II was the replacement of the Merlin XII with a Merlin 45. This new engine had an improved supercharger with two gears to improve performance at high altitude. As would happen several times in the Spitfire development story, the interim version of the aircraft became a major production variant, and the Mk.V remained in production into 1942. Several alterations were made to the design - one significant change was the introduction of the "Universal" wing, with provision for the fitting of 8 .303 machine guns, 4 .303s and 2 x 20mm cannon, or 4 x 20mm cannon. This variation was designated the Mk.Vc Another change was the replacement on some aircraft of the elliptical wingtips with clipped tips. These improved the roll rate to the detriment of the aircraft's stalling speed and high altitude performance.

By the time production ended, over 20,000 Spitfires had been built, and the aircraft had changed engine, its loaded weight had doubled and its maximum speed increased by 90 miles per hour. Despite these changes, the Spitfire of 1945 is instantly recognisable as part of the same family as the prototype of 1936.

The family resemble can be traced even further back, to the S series of racing seaplanes, designed by Reginald J Mitchell in the late 1920s for the Schneider Trophy. In 1931 one S.6 seaplane won the trophy outright, while another raised the world air speed record to 407 mph. However, the Spitfire we know did not develop directly from the seaplanes.

Between them came the Supermarine Type 224. This aircraft was developed in response to an Air Ministry specification (F.7/30), issued in 1931. This called for a fighter to replace the Bristol Bulldog. Mitchell produced a monoplane with a low gull wing, open cockpit and fixed landing gear. It used a Rolls-Royce Goshawk engine, capable of producing 660 hp. Neither Mitchell nor the Air Ministry were entirely satisfied with this aircraft, and the contest was won by the Gloster Gladiator, which would become the last biplane fighter used by the RAF

Mitchell continued to work on his fighter design. The Type 224 developed into the Type 300. This aircraft also used the Rolls-Royce Goshawk, but it was at this stage that the familiar Spitfire wings first appeared. The Type 300 was designed around an Air Ministry specification of 1934 (F.5/34), but the ministry was still not interested. It was only when the board of Vickers, who by now owned Supermarine, matched Mitchell's aircraft with the new Rolls-Royce PV 12 engine (more famous as the Merlin) that the Air Ministry became interested. On 3 January 1935 Supermarine were given a contract to produce a prototype of the new design. Specification F.37/34 was written to describe the new aircraft (at about the same time, specification F.36/34 was based around the new Hawker Hurricane).

Spitfire IX.

Work on the prototype took over a year. It was during this process that R.J. Mitchell showed his genius, refining the initial design of the Type 300 until the almost hand-built prototype was ready. The new aircraft was a very modern design. After a series of arguments within the Air Ministry it was armed with eight .303 Browning machine guns. It had an all-metal stressed-skin and metal wings, with fabric covered control surfaces. The only out-dated element of the aircraft was its two blade fixed pitch wooden propeller.

In the mid 1930s it was not at all clear how combat between monoplane fighters would develop. The Spitfire and the Hurricane represented two alternative possibilities. The Hurricane was fast, but its main strength was its manoeuvrability and turning circle. Likewise, although the Spitfire was agile and manoeuvrable, its main strength was speed. It would soon become clear that Mitchell had followed the correct route (another alternative led to the turret armed Boulton Paul Defiant).

Vickers-Supermarine design team, 1936, relaxes around R.J's car at Eastleigh after the maiden flight of Spitfire K5054.

18

The prototype was built around a Merlin "C" engine, providing 990 hp. It first flew on 5 March 1936 in the hands of Vicker's chief test pilot, Captain J "Mutt" Summers. The aircraft was fast, capable of close to 350 mph in level flight. Only four months earlier the Hawker Hurricane had seemed astonishingly quick at 315 mph, while the contemporary Bf 109B could only reach 298 mph.

The Spitfire is often described as being a small aircraft – one German visitor dismissed it as a "toy". In fact it was four feet wider and 18 inches longer than its most famous opponent, the Bf 109. If the original production version – the Bf 109C - had still been in use in 1940, then the battle between them would have been very one-sided. It is a tribute to Mitchell's design skills that the first version of the Spitfire was an equal for the third major version of the Bf 109.

Mitchell was present to watch the maiden flight of the Spitfire. However, his health was not robust. He had had a brush with cancer in 1933, and in 1937 it returned. On 11 June 1937 Mitchell died, aged only 42. By the time he died, the Spitfire was already famous. It had made its public debut on 27 June 1936 at the Royal Air Force Pageant at Hendon. Earlier in the month (3 June), Supermarine had received an order for 310 production Spitfires.

Mitchell was succeeded in charge of the Spitfire project by Joseph Smith, who had been the chief draughtsman on the project. It was Smith who would evolve the Spitfire through over twenty models and six years of war, making sure that it would always be able to respond to any new German threat.

The Mk V was produced in greater numbers than any other single mark of Spitfire. It was the main version of the fighter during 1941, replacing the Mk I and II in service in time to take part in the first British counterattacks over France. During the summer of 1941 it held an advantage over the Bf 109, but in September 1941 the Fw 190 made its operation debut, and the Mk V found itself outclassed. Despite this, it remained the main RAF fighter until the summer of 1942, and the low level LF.Mk V remained in use into 1944.

The Mk V had been designed as an interim mark. The Mk III saw a redesign of the basic fuselage, to carry the more powerful Merlin XX engine. However, that engine was in short supply, and the internal changes in the Mk III would have delayed production. Rolls-Royce had continued work on the Merlin, producing the Merlin 45. This engine produced 1,515 hp at 11,000 feet. It could easily fit in a Mk I or II fuselage, allowing aircraft already under production to be converted to the new standard. Later in the run the similar Merlin 46, 50 and 50A engines were also used in the Mk V. However, while the Merlin XX had a two speed supercharger (one for low altitude and one of high altitude), the Merlin 45 only had the high altitude supercharger.

The first Mk V was produced in January 1941, and tests proved it to be very nearly as good as the Mk III, but without the extra complexity involved in that version. In March 1941 it was decided to produce the Mk V instead of the Mk III. The type had already entered production by this stage, with No. 92 squadron being the first to receive it in February 1941.

Production was initially divided between the Va with the eight machine gun "a" wing (94 built) and the Vb with the "b" wing of two 20mm cannon and four machine guns. Its main opponent over the summer of 1941 would be the Bf 109F. This was probably the best version of the Bf 109 fighter, and very similar to the Spitfire V. This time it was the Spitfire that was better at high altitude and the Bf 109 at low altitude, and the Spitfire Vb that was the more heavily armed (the Bf 109F-2 carried one 15mm cannon and two 7.9mm (.311 inch) machine guns). However, in 1941 the Mk V was used in the various types of missions over France, known as "leaning over the channel", which saw Spitfire losses mount for little practical return. This time it was the RAF that lost every pilot shot down, with many experienced pilots being taken into captivity on these missions.

In October 1941 the Mk Vc appeared. This used the universal "c" wing developed for the Mk III, which could carry either eight machine guns, four 20mm cannon or two cannon and four machine guns. The two cannon/ four machine gun combination was most common, as the four cannon version was significantly heavier, reducing performance.

The Mk V saw the first appearance of the F (fighter) and LF (Low level Fighter) designations. LF Mk Vs used modified Merlin 45M, 50M and 55M engines that produced their best power at lower altitudes. With the appearance of the LF Mk V, the standard Mk V became the F. Mk V. The LF Mk V could reach 355 mph at 5,900 feet, making it as quick as the Fw 190 and faster than the Bf 109G. The Mk V also saw the introduction of drop tanks to carry extra fuel, initially a 30 gallon model and later a 80 gallon version. It was also the first Spitfire to be adapted to carry bombs.

The Fw 190 appeared in September 1941, and outclassed the Spitfire V. Several changes were made to the Mk V to improve its chances against the new German fighter while the RAF waited for the improved Mk IX, VI or VII to arrive. One of the most

Spitfire Mark VB fighters of No. 131 Squadron RAF at Merston, West Sussex, England, United Kingdom, June 1942.

significant was the long awaited arrival of a carburettor designed to work properly under negative-G, which much improved the dog fighting ability of the Mk V. Despite these changes, the Fw 190 remained a superior aircraft On 1 June 1942 during a raid on northern Belgium the Fw 190s shot down eight Spitfires for no lose. The next day another raid suffered just as badly, when seven Spitfires were shot down for no return. Raids over northern Europe would have to wait for the arrival of the Mk IX.

The Mk V was the first Spitfire to be used in large numbers outside Britain. The first such deployment came on 7 March 1942, when fifteen Mk Vbs were delivered to Malta in Operation Spotter. This operation also saw the Spitfire launched from an aircraft carrier. On Malta the Spitfire was used to hold off the Bf 109F, while the Hurricane attacked the lower level bombers. Loses were heavy. Despite a second delivery of Spitfires on 21 March, by the end of 23 March there were only five serviceable fighters on Malta. HMS Eagle, the carrier used to deliver them had now been damaged, and so the next attempt to reinforce Malta was launched by the U.S.S. Wasp. This time 46 Spitfire Vcs were ferried to Malta on 13 April in Operation Calendar. Sadly, many of these aircraft were destroyed in German bombing raids, launched to coincide with their arrival. It would take one more major supply effort, Operation Bowery, to properly boost the defences of Malta. This time sixty Spitfires reached Malta, and the island was ready for them. The same Spitfires that had just flown in were now scrambled to deal with the inevitable incoming raid. Operation Bowery helped to ensure the survival of Malta, thus playing a major role in the successful allied campaigns in North Africa.

The second overseas theatre to receive the Spitfire was North Africa. The delivery route to Egypt saw aircraft shipped to the west coast of Africa, and then flown across the continent in ten stages to Egypt. This was a slow route, and the first Spitfire squadron only became operation in May 1941. This was just in time to take part in the retreat to Egypt in the summer of 1941. After that the Spitfire Vc took part in the air battles that accompanied the battle of El Alamein, flying top cover to protect ground attack aircraft from the Bf 109Fs of the German desert air force. Their presence helped maintain allied air superiority over the battlefield.

The Mk V also saw service in the Far East. Three squadrons were based at Darwin, on the northern coast of Australia from January 1943. The several conditions they faced at Darwin did not suit the Spitfire, which suffered a series of mechanical problems in the hot humid tropical environment. Despite these problems, the Spitfire proved itself able to catch the Mitsubishi Ki-46 "Dinah" reconnaissance aircraft, which had previously been too high and too fast to be caught by the aircraft previously in northern Australia. The Spitfire V's tropical filters caused a significant deterioration in performance, the aircraft themselves had suffered on the long voyage, and their condition worsened in part because spare parts were rare. The Mk V had a short combat career in India. Three squadrons moved to the Burma front in November 1943, but in February 1944 they were replaced by the Mk VIII, which was exclusively used in the Mediterranean and Far Eastern theatres.

The Mk III was the first major redesign of the Spitfire. The new aircraft was based around the Merlin XX engine, a 1240 horse power engine with a two-speed supercharger, which would have given much better high altitude performance.

Other changes included a shorter clipped wing, which reduced the wingspan to 32'7", increasing the rate of roll. The bulletproof glass on the canopy was moved inside the cockpit, reducing drag. The tail wheel was made retractable. The universal "c" wing was used, which could take four 20mm cannon, eight .303in machine guns, or two cannon and four machine guns. Maximum speed increased to 385 mph.

However, although an order was placed for mass production of the Mk III, it was soon cancelled. The Merlin XX was in short supply, and was needed more urgently in the Hurricane II.

Meanwhile, Rolls Royce had developed the Merlin 45, a similar engine that could be used in a Mk I or Mk II fuselage. The Mk III was abandoned in favour of the Mk V, although many of the improvements first seen in the Mk III were used in later versions of the aircraft. The Mk III airframe was later used to test the Merlin 61 engine, becoming the ancestor of the Mk VII, VIII and IX Spitfires.

The Mk VI Spitfire was a high altitude fighter, designed to deal with the threat posed by very high flying *Luftwaffe* aircraft, especially the Junkers Ju86. The Mk VI used the same airframe as the Mk V, but with a Merlin 47 engine, providing 1,415hp and a

A view of the Spitfire XII from below, clearly showing the clipped wings.

four bladed propeller. The most distinctive feature of this version of the Spitfire was its extended wingtips, designed to increase its performance at high altitude. Ninety-Seven Mk VIs were built between December 1941 and October 1942. Six were sent to the Middle East, while the rest remained in Britain.

The Mk VI was not a great success. It had a pressurised cockpit that had to be locked in place, making it unpopular with the pilots. Its performance was not as impressive as had been hoped – in the Middle East it was outperformed by modified Mk Vs. Finally, the threat of high altitude German bombers did not materialise. The surviving Mk VIs were removed from front line service, and used as training aircraft. In this role the pressurised cockpit, extended wing tips and guns were all removed. The idea of a high altitude pressurised Spitfire had not been abandoned. Production of the Mk VI overlapped with that of the Mk VII, which began in August 1942.

1942 - THE FIGHT CONTINUES

At the beginning of 1942, Fighter Command had 60 squadrons of Spitfires. The Fw-190 was first encountered in quantity during operations in connection with the dash through the English Channel by the warships Scharnhorst and Gneisenau from Brest to Wilhelmshaven on 12 February 1942. Despite being aware of the imminence of the break-out, a combination of bad weather and unserviceabilities in the patrolling aircraft had given the Germans a head start. The ships were eventually discovered by a section of Spitfires of 91 Squadron, and by the Senior Air Staff Officer of No 11 Group, Group Captain Victor Beamish, who was aloft in another Spitfire. Spitfires subsequently fought a series of running battles with Fw-190s and Bf-109s.

The Fw-190's advantage came from its powerful BMW engine and its high-rate of roll. The Spitfire Mk V was finding itself outmatched, and 59 were lost in April. In May, the Bf-109G appeared, optimised for high-level operations. The first of 100 Spitfire Mk VIs had entered into service in April with No 616 Squadron, intended for high-altitude operations where the Bf-109 had previously reigned supreme. In response to the introduction of the Fw-190, another 'interim' mark of Spitfire was proposed, pending full scale development of the Mk VIII. The result was the Mk IX. Like the Mk V, this 'stop-gap' was also an outstanding success, 5,665 being built, the second highest number of any mark!

In June, an Fw-190 landed at Pembrey after its pilot had become lost. This gave the RAF an early opportunity to test the aircraft against the Spitfire Mk V, and it proved superior in all respects except for turning ability. Pending the arrival of the Spitfire Mk IX, some Mk Vs had their wing tips removed, decreasing the span by four feet four inches. The 'clipped-wing' Spitfire was marginally faster than the standard Mk V but had a considerably better rate of roll. A Merlin with a modified supercharger was also fitted, which gave a speed at low level equivalent to that of the Fw-190. Such Spitfires were known as 'clipped and cropped'.

The first Spitfire Mk IXs went to No 64 Squadron at Hornchurch in July. When tested against the captured Fw-190, the Mk IX was found to compare favourably. It was just in time. The *Luftwaffe* began to respond to Fighter Command's offensive by mounting very-low-level hit-and-run raids with small numbers of Fw-190s.

On 19 August, 6,000 Canadian troops were put ashore at Dieppe for a large-scale raid. Code-named Operation Jubilee, the raid was a costly failure but provided invaluable lessons for subsequent seaborne invasions. Of the 67 RAF squadrons committed in support, 48 were of Spitfires - 42 with Mk Vs, four with Mk IXs and two with Mk VIs. Of the 106 Allied aircraft lost, 88 were fighters, most of them Spitfires.

On 29 September, the RAF's Nos 71, 121 and 133 'Eagle' Squadrons flown by American volunteers became the 334th, 335th and 336th Squadrons of the United States Army Air Force.

Their primary task was to act as escorts to B-17 bombers, a role for which the Spitfire had never been envisaged and for which it was unsuitable.

The Photographic Reconnaissance Unit was split into four squadrons in October. Nos 541, 542 and 543 were fully equipped with Spitfire Mk IVs, while 544 Squadron had other types as well as some Mk IVs.

European operations had taken precedence over those in the Middle and Far East theatres. The first overseas deployment of Spitfires as fighters took place on 7 March, when 15 tropicalised Mk Vs carrying 90-gallon slipper fuel tanks took off from the flight deck of HMS Eagle bound for Malta, 600 miles (960 km) away. Subsequent deliveries in the same manner turned the air battle for Malta in the RAF's favour. One aircraft suffered fuel-feed failure and became the first Spitfire without a hook to land on an aircraft

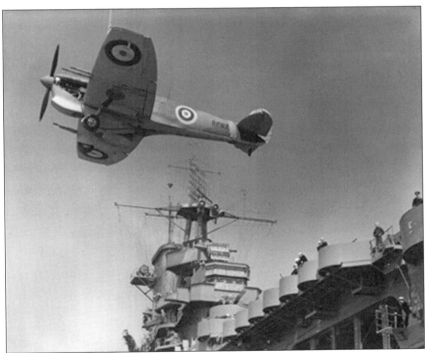

Spitfire Mk. V fighter of No. 603 Squadron RAF being hauled aboard USS Wasp by a crane, Glasgow, Scotland, United Kingdom, 13 April 1942.

carrier. By August, the Spitfire had entirely taken over the air defence of Malta. To relieve the aircraft carriers from their ferry role, Spitfire Mk VCs were fitted with an extra internal 29-gallon tank and an external jettisonable 170-gallon tank. Armament was reduced to two machine guns. In this form, the aircraft were able to fly the 1,100 miles (1,750 km) from Gibraltar to Malta, where the extra tanks were removed and the armament refitted. These flights commenced in October. Malta-based Spitfires of 126 Squadron were the first to carry two 250lb bombs, which they did during operations over Sicily.

The first Desert Air Force squadron to receive Spitfires was No 145 in April 1942. These were tropicalised Mk VBs. One was stripped of armour and two 0.5-inch machine guns replaced the normal armament. Fitted with a four-bladed propeller and with its Merlin suitably 'tweaked' to give more power at high altitude, this aircraft climbed to 42,000 feet to shoot down a Ju-86P reconnaissance aircraft. Subsequently, Ju-86Ps were intercepted and brought down from heights of 45,000 and 50,000 feet.

The Seafire was first in action during the Allied invasion of Morocco and Algeria when a Mk IB of No 801 Squadron from HMS Furious shot down a Dewoitine 520 on 8 November. American Spitfire Mk VBs were also used during these landings.

The Fw-190 arrived in the Western Desert in November and, the following month, a few Spitfire Mk IXs were attached to 145 Squadron to counter them. Other overseas deployments of Spitfires had seen three Mk IVs being sent to Vaenga, in North Russia, to keep on eye on German warships. While there, they carried Soviet markings.

Pending availability of the PR Mk XI, 15 Mk IXs were modified for PR work. They were first used operationally in November by No 541 Squadron.

- CHAPTER 2 -
THE SPITFIRE

ON MARCH 5th, 1936, the first Spitfire designed by R.J. Mitchell, was flown by, Captain Joseph Summers, at Eastleigh Aerodrome, Southampton, England.

The Spitfire and her partner the Hurricane won a unique battle for this country's survival.

The Battle of Britain is said to have lasted from the 1st of July 1940 to the end of October. The *Luftwaffe's* aim was the destruction of the will and ability to resist invasion. Radar and plotting rooms guided the British fighters to the invaders, sometimes 300 to 500 strong.

The bombers flew at 20,000 feet; they were sitting ducks for the fighters. But the escorting Me.109 could be lurking above waiting to dive out of the sun and bunch the British.

Air Vice Marshall Johnnie Johnson suggests, "There is no way Goring could have set about the Battle of Britain a lot differently. I don't think he was a professional like our Commander in Chief. He didn't appreciate the importance of Radars, which had the effects of multiplying our squadrons. We had 14 radar stations from the wash down to the Isle of Wight. Only one of which was bombed during the Battle of Britain. Radar Stations were the eyes of fighter pilots."

Group Captain Douglas Bader adds, "Somebody saw the enemy, they seemed a long way away and quite small. When you got a bit smarter, you didn't rush to overtake them. You found that the little dot, or the airplane rushed straight at you because your going to fast. You had no chance of shooting.

You didn't rush it. The ideal way to shoot an aeroplane down was at the same speed and about 200 yards behind it.

In other words you had maximum time, there was no hurry. That was the secret. Not to rush.

For most of us, it was purely just the aeroplane we wanted to get rid of. We didn't are a bit whether the chap inside got out or was killed.

We disliked the iron crosses and the crocked sign of the Swastika, and anyhow who the hell were these chaps to come over into our sky and drop bombs on us and our people.

Now if your flying an aeroplane, you very much have to be on the ball, alert. Then you discover a whole stream of bullets come in the back of the cockpit. There is nothing you can do about it. But physically your doing something to get out of the way of the streams of stuff coming in behind you. So you're very much on the job, so to speak.

I don't believe you can be frightened or active at the same time. Not in that particular context.

I can't think of anyone who was actually frightened in the aeroplane: flying along in the battle or seeing the battle about to start. Its only when something physical happens to you get this feeling. I can only describe it as a hand clutching my heart. Now if that's fear, then I was frightened."

Spitfires in action during the Battle of Britain.

The Spitfire was formidable but not invincible. Most of the first aircrafts were provided by the factories and repair shops around the Southampton area. But soon reinforcements were on the way from Castle Bromwich near Birmingham. This gigantic factory in Castle Bromwich was built before the war by Nutfield to make aircraft. The factory was in fact designed by the Nutfield organisation just to make Spitfires. Although this factory was fully equip and making parts, and in the early days of 1940, it had yet to produce a Spitfire. But within six weeks of turning it around when orders for greater numbers of Spitfires had been received, the factory, within six weeks, had produced ten.

The employees at the Castle Bromwich factory was a very mixed bag, from footballers to lion tamers and worked long hours to achieve the high level of production. They were said to do a very good job, making a lot of Spitfires. In one period they were producing nearly 400 Spitfires a month, which was a lot of aeroplane for 1940.

At this time the morale of the German bomber crews was severely shaken by heavy losses, but Goering insisted the Me's should stay close to the bomber until attacked. This put them at a tactical disadvantage, with the fighter General Galland told Goering "Then you should give us an outfit of Spitfires" Galland envied the British defences of manoeuvrability.

In September 1940, the *Luftwaffe* attacked the Spitfires in their most vulnerable form: as unfinished fuselages at Southampton.

One Southampton worker Harold smith quotes; "People were so shattered, people were fainting, females screaming everywhere. The whole building was shaking 2-3 inches. We had very little warning, and as I ran up the hill, as we didn't trust the factory shelters, I looked up and saw the Me.110's and I saw one drop a bomb directly above me. I had to decide quickly which way to go. I witnessed the roof of a house completely fly up and fall down, covering us in dust and debris. And within a few moments it was all over. We were just thanking god we were still alive."

Two days later, the bombers returned which lead for Lord Beaverbrook to say thumping the table "I want more Spitfires, more Spitfires and your going to disperse all over the country, complete dispersal."

It was then to find suitable places to build Spitfire's and within six weeks, 35 factories had been found and 16 of those were already working day and night shifts. Production managed to keep ahead of loses.

In 1941, the Spitfires moved to an attacking role, hammering the Germans in France and the low Country's, destroying communication, armour and aircraft on the ground. Hitler was now at war with Russia, but at the end of 1941 the *Luftwaffe* sent a potent new fighter into battle, with devastating effect.

It was the Focke-Wulf 190. A radial engined fighter which out flew the Spitfire Mk. V in every respect.

The air ministry at this point in time asked for a combined operation to capture a FW 190 in order to appraise it. Test Pilot "Geoffrey Quill" was called in.

"We were going to be put ashore and have the army put us into a German field. The army had to get me into a FW 190 with the engine running. If that was to be the case, I knew I had just more than 50/50 to get the FW 190 off and out the airfield"

The operation like many missions had a surprising outcome. In fact a FW 190 had landed in a field in Wales. Leaving test pilot Geoffrey Quill quite relived.

Stanely Hooker Rolls Royce quotes; "We originally designed the two stage Merlin, the final merlin engine to fit the high altitude Wellingborough bomber, and that's how we stated, but the mechanical liability of the engine had to be dealt with: the bearings, the conrods, pistons and the engine block to take this increase in power. And we got this engine going when Hieves said what would happen if we that into a Spitfire. None of us had thought about that. It made a huge modification to the Spitfire as the engine was 9 inches longer, so the whole thing had to be moved forward. We put the first two stage Merlin 61 in the Spitfire and flew it. We had this tremendous increase in performance.

I remember the pilot telling me, he climbed up past a Focke-Wulf 190, they were both climbing and the Spitfire passed the FW. He remembers the look of astonishment on the German pilots face as he followed this Spitfire going up past him.

Air Vice Marshall Johnnie Johnson add; "The beauty of the Spitfire 9 was it was almost the same as its predecessors, it was hard to distinguish in the air, between the Spitfire 5 and Spitfire 9, and often the Germans would come rushing at us thinking it was a 5, it was great to see when they realised they were mistaken."

"One day over France, when I was leading the Canadian wing, we got split up. I eventually went down to ground level and I climbed back to about 14,000 feet, when I rejoined what I thought be a flight with my Canadians in six Spitfire 9's. I said across to them "rejoin, I am pulling up in front of you" with no response, I soon realised it was in fact six Focke-Wulf 190's, all I got was a shower of shoots from them. But it says a lot for the Spitfire that I am here alive today, telling this story"

Nicknamed BONDOWOSO, Spitfire MK. Vb serial no. BL676 started its life as ordinary series-production fighter, but came to play a pivotal role in the development of the Seafire, a seaborne variant of Supermarine's legendary aircraft.

SEAFIRES

The Spitfires went to sea as Seafires; some were fitted with folding wings and remained in service long after the war.

Spitfires flew from aircraft carriers to defend water and weren't action within 30 minutes of landing, they covered the invasion of North Africa and every Amphibious operation thereafter.

After D-day one aircraft even carried emergency supplies of Beer to France.

In 1944, there was almost a second Battle of Britain against the v-weapons. The V-1 Flying bomb was a brilliant use of RAM jet, an automatic pilot and speed most outstripping our latest fighters.

Spitfires could just catch them out of a dive and destroy the,: at considerable risk to the pilot.

THE FIGHTING SPITFIRE: A SHORT DESCRIPTION OF BRITAIN'S FAMOUS FIGHTING AEROPLANE

The chief attribute of the singe- seat fighting aeroplane is speed. It was the speediest man carrying war machine in existence in the early 1940's achieving speeds of up to 400mph.

And it is because they must be able to fly so fast that they must be made so small. The smaller the quicker. They are masterpieces of compression. If you saw a list of the bits and pieces that make up a fighter you would imagine that they would fill the Albert Hall. Yet, in the interests of speed, they are all squeezed into the space of a cupboard. To take the Spitfire as an example-the span is 11ft 5", the length about 30ft and the height about 11ft 6".

Apart from the elaborate accessories and equipment, there are four chief fighter ingredients: a man, a sheaf of guns, a huge engine and a small airframe. The aeroplane is built to a close fit round the man who works it. There is only just room for his shoulders. To someone not used to it it would feel tight under the arms. Looked at from the front it appears like a dot with a couple of fine lines out to the right and left. From the sides it looks like a cigar- not those expensive parallel-sided cigars, but one of the small ones which taper more to one end than the other.

The engine itself is compressed. More than 1000 horsepower – which I believe is about the power of a big railway locomotive- is stuffed into the space of a cabin trunk. The pilot is crammed up close behind this powerful piece of machinery.

The wings are as slim and small as they can be made, provided they give enough lift for the weight. But although they are small they have to accommodate the undercarriage, which tucks itself away into them when the aeroplane is in the air, and the eight machine guns, four in each wing.

An all the ingenuity of compression is designed to get that one man and his eight guns through the air at the highest possible speed. His safety and success depend on speed. So the fighter must give speed, all the speed which aviation knowledge and experience can find.

- CHAPTER 3 -
THE SPITFIRE MARKS

AFTER THE development of the first Spitfire, the aircraft underwent a number of major improvements, or marks, so that by the end of World War Two, the Spitfire Mark XIX was a very different proposition to the aircraft that had first entered service. The first aircraft that can be classed as a Spitfire was the prototype – K5054, which first flew in July 1934. Only one was built. By June 1936 the Spitfire Mark 1 was in testing – it was this aircraft, along with the Hurricane, that fought in the early days of the Battle of Britain.

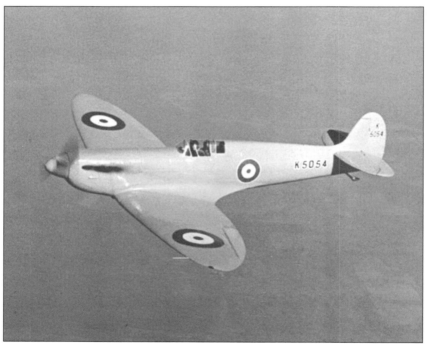

5 March 1936: Vickers Aviation chief test pilot, Captain Joseph ("Mutt") Summers, CBE (1904–1954), makes the first flight of the prototype of the legendary Supermarine Spitfire, K5054, at Eastleigh Aerodrome, Southampton, England. Landing after only 8 minutes, he said, "Don't change a thing!"

K5054

- **Total built:** 1. In testing July 1934.Vickers-Supermarine Type 300.

- **Production Head of Design Team:** Reginald J. Mitchell (until d.1937), Joseph Smith

- **Design Office:** Supermarine Aviation Works (Vickers) Ltd, Woolaston, Southampton

- **Role:** Interceptor fighter

- **Crew:** One

- **Engine:** One liquid cooled, 12 cylinder Vee, Rolls-Royce Merlin C 990 hp (738 kW). Later fitted with Merlin F 1,035 hp (772 kW) and then Merlin II 1,030 hp (768 kW).

- **Armament:** None initially. Later eight 0.303 in (7.7 mm) Browning machine-guns in wings, with 300 rounds per gun.

- **Dimensions:**
    Length - 29 ft 11 in (9.12 m)
    Height (to tip of prop) - 12 ft 8 in (3.86 m)
    Wing Span - 36 ft 10 in (11.23 m)
    Wing Area - 242.0 sq ft (22.48 sq m)

- **Weights:**
    Empty (Tare) - 4,082 lb (1854 kg)
    Fully Loaded - 5,359 lb (2,434 kg)

- **Performance:**
    Maximum level speed - 349 mph at 16,800 ft
    Initial rate of climb - 2400 ft/min (731 m/min)
    Time to 15,000 ft - (4,570 m) 5 min 52 sec
    Service ceiling - 35,400 ft (10,790 m)
    Endurance - 1.78 hr

MARK I

- **Total built:** 1,577. In service from June 1936 to August 1940.

- **Engine:** Rolls-Royce Merlin II or III

- **Performance:**
  Maximum power - 1,030 hp
  Maximum speed - 362 mph at 18,500 feet
  Service ceiling - 34,500 feet
  Rate of climb - 2,195 feet per minute

- **Armament:**
  8 x .303 Browning Mark II machine guns (Mark 1A) or
  4 x .303 Mark II machine guns and 2 x 20.mm Hispano
  cannon.

MARK II

- **Total built**: 920. First flew in 1939.

- **Engine:** Rolls-Royce Merlin C liquid-cooled 27 litre V12

- **Performance:**
  Maximum power - 900 hp
  Maximum speed - 349 mph at 16,800 feet
  Service ceiling - 34,500 feet
  Rate of climb - 1,770 feet per minute

- **Armament:** 8 x .303 Browning Mark II machine guns

The Mark II was very similar to the Mark 1 with a few modifications.

MARK III

- **Total built:** 2

The Mark III was a complete reworking of the Spitfire. Making its maiden flight on August 15th 1940, with a top speed of 400 mph, it was unpopular with test pilots and all orders were cancelled.

MARK IV

This was the first prototype with a Griffon engine. With a top speed of 470 mph it was armed with 6 x 20mm cannon. It first flew on November 27th 1941. The Mark IV later became the Mark XII.

PR IV

The Spitfire PR IV was the first photoreconnaissance Spitfire. Powered by a Merlin engine, it was stripped of anything that was considered to be excess weight – including weaponry – but carried an extra fuel load (up to a maximum of 247 gallons) and either one or two cameras.

MARK V

- **Total built:** 6,787. First flew in August 1939. In service from August 1939 to October 1941.

- **Engine:** Rolls-Royce Merlin 45, 45M, 46, 50, 50M + 56

- **Performance:**
  Maximum power - 1,440 to 1,470hp
  Maximum speed - 371 mph at 20,000 feet
  Service ceiling - 37,500 feet
  Rate of climb - 2,440 feet per minute

- **Armament:** 4 x .303 Browning Mark II machine guns and 2 x 20.mm Hispano cannon.

MARK VI

- **Total built:** 97

The Mark VI was a high-altitude interceptor with a pressurised cabin, elongated wings and a ceiling of 39,000 feet. It was designed to combat the new generation of high-altitude German bombers that had been developed. As this threat never occurred, the Mark VI was primarily used as a trainer.

MARK VII

- **Total built:** 140

This was a version built around the Mark VI. It had a maximum ceiling of 43,000 feet. Its 1,710-hp Merlin engine gave it a maximum speed of 408 mph.

MARK VIII

- **Total built:** 1,654. First flew in January 1942.

The Mark VIII was built as an all-round interceptor. The Mark VIII saw service in the Mediterranean and Far East conflicts. A few Mark VIII's (6) were fitted with a Griffon engine and were used as prototypes for the Mark XIV. A version of the Mark VIII became a two-seater trainer.

PR VIII

This Spitfire was an advanced version of the photoreconnaissance Spitfire. 70 were built in 1942.

MARK IX

- **Total built:** 5,665. First flew October 1941.

- **Engine:** Rolls-Royce Merlin 61, 63, 65A or 66

- **Performance:**
    Maximum power - 1,475 to 1,650hp
    Maximum speed - 408 mph at 25,000 feet
    Service ceiling - 43,000 feet
    Rate of climb - 3,950 feet per minute

- **Armament:** 4 x .303 Browning Mark II machine guns and 2 x 20.mm Hispano cannon.

MARK X

- **Total built:** 16. First flew May 1942.

This was an unarmed photoreconnaissance aircraft, which was pressurised. A retractable tail-wheel aided streamlining and reduced fuel consumption.

MARK XI

- **Total built:** 464. First flew August 1941.

The Mark XI became the RAF's principal photoreconnaissance aircraft in the later stages of World War Two. It had a specially smoothed airframe that gave a top speed of 417 mph at 24,200 feet. On April 27th 1944, a Mark XI flew at Mach 0.89 in a dive.

MARK XII

- **Total built:** 100. First flew in August 1941.

The Mark XII was the first Griffon engine powered Spitfire to enter service with the RAF. It was used as a low-level interceptor and was especially successful against V1's.

MARK XIII

- **Total built:** 26. First flew in August 1942.

The Mark XIII was a low-level photoreconnaissance aircraft and later flew with the Fleet Air Arm.

MARK XIV

- **Total built:** 957. First flew in July 1942.

- **Engine:** Rolls-Royce Griffon 65 37-litre liquid cooled V12

- **Performance:**
    Maximum power - 2,035
    Maximum speed - 439 mph at 24,500 feet
    Service ceiling - 43,000 feet
    Rate of climb - 4,580 feet per minute

- **Armament:** 4 x .303 Browning Mark II machine guns and 2 x 20.mm Hispano cannon.

MARK XVI

- **Total built:** 1,053. First flew in May 1942.

The Mark XVI was essentially a low-level interceptor of the Mark IX powered by a Packard-built 1,580 hp Merlin 266.

MARK XVIII

- **Total built:** 300. First flew December 1942.

- **Performance:** Maximum speed - 437 mph.

Saw service in the Far East but right towards the end of World War Two. Flown during the 1948 Arab-Israeli War.

MARK XIX

- **Total built:** 225. First flew in June 1943.

A photoreconnaissance aircraft powered by a Griffon engine. The XIX had a top speed of 460 mph and it was the last Spitfire Mark to be flown in the RAF.

F 20

- **Total built:** 2. First flew in April 1942.

The F 20 was a prototype for a number of future F versions all powered by a Griffon engine.

F 21

- **Total built:** 121 . First flew in March 1942.

This version was so troubled that the Air Ministry made it clear that they believed that the Spitfire had reached the end of the line with regards to production. All 121 aircraft were powered by a Griffon engine but some were fitted with contra-rotating six-bladed propellers.

F 22

- **Total built:** 264. First flew in June 1942.

This was the successful version of the F 21. It entered service with the RAF in 1946 and flew until 1955. Capable of 449 mph at 25,000 feet. However, jet technology had taken over and the days of propeller-powered fighters were all but over. One F 23 was built.

F 24

Total built: 78. First flew in June 1943.

Engine: Rolls-Royce Griffon 61, 64 or 85

Performance:
> Maximum power - 2,340 hp
> Maximum speed - 454 mph at 26,000 feet
> Service ceiling - 43,000 feet
> Rate of climb - 4,100 feet per minute

Armament: 4 x 20.mm Hispano Mk II cannon plus under wing-mounted rockets.

Mark	Role	Engine Type	Weight (lbs)	Max Speed (mph)	Range (Miles)	Ceiling (ft)
IA	Fighter	Merlin II or III	5332	367	-	-
IB	Fighter	Merlin III	5784	-	-	-
IIA	Fighter	Merlin XII	6317	-	-	-
IIB	Fighter	Merlin XII	6527	-	-	-
P.R. IV	Photo Reconnaissance	Merlin 45/46	7178	372	1460	38000
VA	Fighter	Merlin 45/46	6417	369	-	37500
VB	Fighter	Merlin 45/46	6622	369	480	37500
VC	Fighter	Merlin 45/46	6785	369	470	37500
F.V1	Fighter	Merlin 47	6797	364	475	40000
F.VII	Fighter	Merlin 61/64	7875	408	660	43000
H.F.VII	High altitude fighter	Merlin 71	7875	416	660	44000
P.R.VII	Photo Reconnaissance	Merlin 45/46	6585	369	710	37000
F.VIII	Fighter and bomber	Merlin 61/63/63A	7767	408	660	43000
L.F.VIII	Low altitude fighter	Merlin 66	7767	404	660	41500
H.F.VIII	High altitude fighter	Merlin 70	7767	416	660	44000
F.IX	Fighter	Merlin 61/63	7300	400	434	40000
L.F.IX	Low alt fighter	Merlin 66	7300	404	434	42500
H.F.IX	High alt fighter	Merlin 64/70	7300	416	434	45000
P.R.X	Photo Reconnaissance	Merlin 61/63/63A/70	8159	416	1370	43000
P.R.XI	Photo Reconnaissance	Griffon III or IV	7872	422	1200	44000
F.XII	Fighter and bomber	Merlin 32	7280	393	329	40000
P.R.XIII	Photo Reconnaissance	Merlin 65	6364	348	500	38000
F.XIV	Fighter	Griffon 65	8490	450	460/620	40000
F.XVI	Low alt fighter/bomber	Merlin 266	7300	400	434	40000

- CHAPTER 4 -

THE DEVELOPMENT OF THE ROLLS-ROYCE MERLIN ENGINE

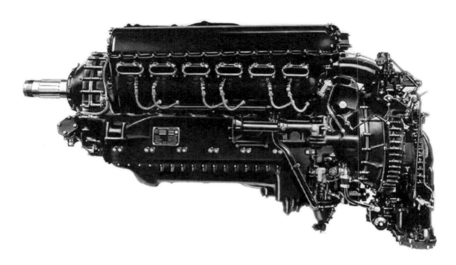

The Rolls-Royce Merlin III

ONE OF the British technical achievements, which proved most important for the country's war effort, was the Rolls-Royce Merlin engine. It not only powered the Spitfire, but also the Hurricane, Lancaster, Mosquito and the Mustang, together with some variants of the Halifax, Beaufighter and Wellington. The vast majority of Spitfires produced were fitted with various variants of the Merlin. Even today the Merlin is one of the most renowned piston aero engines of all time.

The design of the Merlin owns much to the company's most successful aero engine of the early 1930s, the Rolls-Royce Kestrel. The Kestrel was a successful inline V-12 engine which provided excellent service on a number of RAF aircraft of the period. Most particularly, it was selected to power the entire family of highly successful and acclaimed family of Hawker biplanes, the Hart,

Audax, Demon, Hardy, Hind and Osprey two-seaters and Fury and Nimrod fighters, the aircraft which had a prominent role during the RAF's inter-war period.

The Kestrel was Rolls-Royce's first cast-block engine. Earlier aero engine designs had used individually machined steel cylinders that were screwed onto a crankcase, whereas the cast-block design used a single block of aluminium that was machined to form cylinders. The result was both simpler to build as well as lighter and more reliable, requiring only an investment in new machining equipment.

The third key advance in the Kestrel was the use of a pressurized cooling system. Water boils at 100°C at standard atmospheric pressure, but this temperature decreases with altitude. As it does so its ability to carry heat away from the engine drops, to the point where at high altitudes a gigantic radiator needs to be used to cool it again. The solution was to pressurise the entire cooling system, thereby not only preventing the drop in cooling performance with altitude, but in fact increasing the boiling point even on the ground. The Kestrel was built to maintain enough pressure to keep the boiling point at about 150°C.

The Kestrel was first produced in 1927 at 450 hp, which soon improved in the IB model to 525 hp. This model saw widespread use in the famed Hawker Hart family that dominated British air power during the early 1930s. However it was not long before line improvements increased power dramatically; the V model provided 695 hp at 3,000 rpm with no basic change to the design, while the XVI used in the Miles Master delivered 745 hp. In 1935, Messerschmitt also tested its Messerschmitt Bf 109 V1 prototype monoplane fighter with Kestrel engine.

Increased availability of higher octane better quality aviation fuels in the late 1930s, allowed the engine to be boosted to even higher power levels without suffering from ping, (detonation) and the Kestrel eventually topped out at 1,050 hp (780 kW) in the Kestrel XXX model of 1940.

THE PEREGRINE

In the early 1930s, Rolls-Royce started planning for the future of its aero engine development programmes and eventually settled on pursuing two main designs. The 700-horsepower Rolls-Royce Peregrine was to be an updated, supercharged development of the existing 22 litre Rolls-Royce Kestrel. Two Peregrines bolted together on a common crankshaft into an X-24 layout would create the 1,700 hp 44 litre Rolls-Royce Vulture for use in larger and heavier aircraft such as bombers.

There was also the possibility that the famous 36-litre 'R' engine from the Supermarine racing planes, itself a development of the Rolls-Royce Buzzard, could be developed into a 1,500 hp-class engine, a sort of scaled-up Kestrel. This line design materialized only much later, leading the Rolls-Royce Griffon.

Initial development of the Peregrine promised to be very successful. However, the Peregrine-Vulture plan left a large gap between 700 and 1,500 horsepower, and Henry Royce saw the need for a more powerful 12-cylinder engine that would utilise the technology developed from the Kestrel production that was light, powerful and could be fitted to single-engine aircraft.

The company management authorised the project to develop on a new 1,100 hp-class design under the designation PV-12. PV stood for "private venture" as the company received no government money for development of such engine.

PV-12 BECOMES THE MERLIN

The new engine was first run on 15 October 1933 and first flown in April 1935 powering the Hawker Hart biplane. Later on the old the company-owned Hawker Horsley became test bed aircraft for the second prototype engine. In 1936, Rolls-Royce decided to invest in a more flexible flying test bed and the choice fell on Heinkel He 70, high-performance German courier aircraft which also had an enclosed passenger cabin from which several engineers could monitor the engine in flight. One example of He 70G powered with Kestrel V was purchased by Rolls-Royce and subsequently used in the Merlin tests during 1936-1937.

Never resolved problems with the evaporative system manifested themselves with all clarity during trials. The system was notoriously failing during taxiing, when there was no cooling airflow around the condensers and thus the steam could not be cooled quickly enough. Similar problems occurred during climbs at high power, this time for the surplus of heat produced by the engine which exceeded the maximum capacity of the cooling system.

Fortunately, in mid-1930s Prestone in the United States has perfected the use of ethylene glycol as a new and cooling medium, much more efficient than water. As glycol became available, the PV-12 was changed to the conventional liquid cooling system instead.

In 1936, the Air Ministry revised their requirements for new fighter aircraft. One of the most fundamental changes was the requirements for airspeed over 300 mph (480 km/h). This would clearly require an engine with more power than the planned 700 hp of the Peregrine, and having learned about the performance of the new Rolls-Royce engine, the government became instantly interested and decided to fund its subsequent development. It is then that the engine received the name Merlin. The name came from the bird – a small falcon also known as "pigeon hawk" – rather than King Arthur's legendary magician. However, in the film The First of the Few, Sir Henry Royce refers to King Arthur's Merlin rather than the bird, but his could be due to some propaganda purposes of the day.

Further modifications to the prototype were designated by capital letters. Thus the Merlin B became the first to use ethylene glycol cooling system; further modifications included changes to the cylinder head and cylinder block castings well as to the cooling system.

Merlin C was sufficiently developed to power the prototypes of new metal stressed-skin monoplanes for the RAF. On 6 November 1935 the prototype Hawker Hurricane, took off to its maiden flight, powered by Merlin C producing 900hp and driving a Watts fixed-pitch two-bladed wooden propeller. This was followed by the Fairey Battle which first flew on 10 March 1936, and the Supermarine Spitfire prototype K5054 on 5 march 1936.

Altogether, Rolls-Royce built and tested at least 33 prototype engines, ending with the production-ready Merlin F. This engine could develop 1,035 hp and was, among other trials, fitted to the Spitfire prototype.

Official RAF photograph taken on 7 June 1944, a day after the invasion in Normandy. It shows rows of factory-fresh Spitfires LF Mk. IXc assembled at a forward repair unit in southern England to replace expected losses of the 2nd Tactical Air Force over the continent. Visible in the far background is an even larger mass of RAF ground vehicles. The mechanics work on the Merlin 66 engine, which is shown to advantage.

MERLIN ENTERS PRODUCTION

The first production version Merlin I was assigned for Fairey Battle production. Only 175 had been built and these were considered to be rather unreliable. As a result, Rolls-Royce introduced an ambitious (TQM) Total Quality Management system to fix the problems. This consisted of taking random engines from the end of assembly line and running them continuously at full power until they failed. Each was then dismantled to find out which part had failed, and that part was redesigned to be stronger. After two years of this programme the Merlin had developed into one of the most reliable aero engines in the world, and could sustain eight-hour combat missions with no problems.

A particular problem with Merlin I was its 'ramp head' where the inlet valves were at a 45-degree angle to the cylinder. This solution was not a success and was replaced with Kestrel-style conventional flat head arrangement wherein the valves are parallel to the cylinder. This modification was designated Merlin II.

The Merlin II was introduced in 1938. After that the production was quickly stepped up. Development of a constant-speed propeller lead to the Merlin III, which was the Merlin II adapted for the use of such propeller and provided with a constant-speed unit.

Merlin II and Merlin III were produced in great numbers, over 9700 in total. These engines powered just about every new RAF aircraft of the period: Hawker Hurricane Mk. I, Supermarine Spitfire Mk. I, Boulton-Paul Defiant Mk. I, Fairey Battle Mk. I, Hawker Henley.

THE ONLY ALTERNATIVE

As it turned out, the Peregrine saw use in only two aircraft, the Westland Whirlwind and the Gloster F9/37 prototype. Although the Peregrine appeared to be a satisfactory design, it was never allowed to fully mature; Rolls-Royce's top priority was then troubleshooting the Merlin. More importantly, the Peregrine did not have the development potential as the Merlin, and the excellent Whirlwind fighter that was powered by a pair of Peregrines was only produced in small quantities.

The Vulture was developed, but proved unreliable owing to excessive problems with lubrication. Consequently, it had a very troubled time in development and two aircraft programmes based on the Vulture, the Avro Manchester bomber and the Hawker Tornado fighter had to be cancelled.

With the Merlin pushing into the 1,500 hp range, the Peregrine and Vulture were both cancelled in 1943.

It was supplanted in service by the Rolls-Royce Griffon which was a development of the R engine. The Griffon only became available in quantity during the last two years of the war.

Britain's second manufacturer of in-line aero engines, Napier, was pursuing the development of 24-cylinder H-pattern engines, of indisputable potential but far greater complexity. Napier Dagger of the 1,000 hp-class was the first engine with this layout and had problems with cooling, maintenance, manufacturing and weight. These problems weren't solved during the Dagger's lifetime. The Dagger powered the Hawker Hector and Handley Page Hereford, both produced in strictly limited numbers and never used operationally.

The 2,000 hp Napier Sabre became available in any numbers during 1942, but the unresolved problems of its predecessor plus unreliable valves dogged its service introduction on the Hawker Typhoon during entire 1943.

Thus it was the Merlin that had to meet all Britain's in-line aero-engine needs for the early war years.

THE MERLIN ENGINE

The Rolls-Royce engines fitted to the Spitfire would be the Merlin XX series.

The Merlin 25 is a 12-cylinder, 60°, V12, liquid cooled engine. It has a compression ratio of 6:1 and its dry weight is 1,430lb.

The two piece cylinder block is cast from aluminum alloy. There are six cylinder liners in each block, manufactured from high carbon steel. Each piston has three compression and two oil scraper rings. The connecting rods are nickel steel forgings, machined to H-sections.

The one-piece-six-throw-crankshaft is machine forged from chrome-molybdenum steel. The crankcase is cast from aluminum alloy. Two inlet and two exhaust valves are fitted to each cylinder head and each exhaust valve had a sodium-cooled stem.

Cylinders

The two cylinders assemblies, mainly the right- and left-hand blocks, are known as the A and B blocks respectively. Each compromises six cylinders, the upper camshaft drive unit and the camshaft and rocker mechanism, which operates the valves incorporated in the cylinders. Each block consists of a separate alloy skirt, head and six detachable wet steel liners which, when bolted together, form the cylinder block proper. In addition to providing part of the coolant jacket, the head also forms the roofs of the sox combustion chambers.

Cylinder Liners

Each cylinder lines is shouldered and spigotted at the upper end to enter its respective recess in the bottom of the cylinder head. The cylinder liner is also provided with a sealing ring at its lower end to form a joint with the crankcase. To which it is drawn by the cylinder holding-down studs.

Cylinder block Covers

The covers are secured to the receptive cylinder blocks by studs and nuts, with a gasket between the two contacting faces. The main difference between A and B covers is that the latter incorporates an engine speed indicator drive whilst former is plain.

Valves

There are two inlet and exhaust valves per cylinder. Both valves are of the trumpet type ad have satellite-ended stems. The valves are not interchangeable. Each valve guide is pressed into its respective bore in the cylinder block until a conical collar near its top end is seated on, and is flush with, the roof of the cylinder block.

Camshaft

A single central camshaft for each cylinder block is mounted in pedestal brackets and operates both on inlet and exhaust valves through rockers fitted with adjustable tappets. The camshafts, which are similar for both blocks, are driven from the wheel case by inclined shafts ending in bevel pinions, which mesh with bevel wheels at the end of the camshaft.

Camshaft auxiliary drive

The air compressor and hydraulic pumps for the turrets are mounted on the rear ends of the A and B cylinder heads. Both are driven from the spur gear wheels attached to the camshaft-driven bevel wheels.

Pistons

The pistons are fully attached to the connecting rods by fully floating gudgeon pins. The connecting rods are of the forked and plain type, the forked rod being fitted to the B-side of the engine.

The pistons machined from light alloy forgings and are fitted with three compression rings above and one grooved scraper ring below the gudgeon pins are made from hollow steel and are retained in the piston by spring wire clips. A pair of oil holes are drilled obliquely and upwards towards the centre to meet in the metal above each gudgeon pin bore to assist in cooling the piston.

- C H A P T E R   5 -
SPITFIRE PRODUCTION

D ELIVERIES OF production Spitfires I's began in June 1938, just over two years after "Mutt" Summers flew the prototype at Southampton on the 5th of March, 1936. In two years preceding production, Supermarine laid out their Woolston factory for large scale production, and organized one of the largest subcontract schemes ever envisioned in Britain. Until that time it was becoming increasingly clear that there was no limit to the likely demand for the Spitfire. It was also obvious that one factory alone was not going to the able to make the demand, even with adequate subcontracting.

Before the war, 'shadow factories' had been created, under the direction of big industrialists such as Lord Nuffield, in readiness to build aircraft when hostilities began. But by the summer of 1940 when Beaverbrook took up his post, the vital Spitfire 'shadow factory' at Castle Bromwich, Birmingham, had yet to produce a single aircraft.

Beaverbrook telephoned Vickers-Supermarine, manufacturers of the Spitfire, and told them to take over Castle Bromwich from the Nuffield Organization, which had been running it, and to forget about the Air Ministry's orders that Castle Bromwich must also tool up for Wellington and Halifax bombers.

In 1938, after the crisis at Munich, Britain introduced the Civilian Repair Organisation or CRO as it became known. Lord Nuffield was placed in charge. The task was that in the event of war workshops had to be organized to accommodate and repair damaged aircraft. Methods of retrieval had to be organized and storage areas where spare parts from destroyed aircraft could be systematically stored and despatched whenever needed. When Churchill appointed Beaverbrook to his ministerial position, he transferred the CRO to Beaverbrook's authority. Again, a war of words developed between the Air Ministry and Lord Beaverbrook. The Air Ministry claiming that all aircraft in storage units were their responsibility and should be under their control. Beaverbrook argued the point that he was the minister responsible for the allocation of aircraft, and that they would be placed where they would be most needed.

Beaverbrook then sent some of his men to padlock all the hangars that contained aircraft in storage and those that contained important and essential spare parts, and enthused by what he had done sent a message to the Air Ministry stating that he was going to store fighter aircraft in Winchester Cathedral !!

Special 'low loaders' were built to carry damaged aircraft back to the CRO. Those damaged beyond repair were stripped and all usable parts and placed in 'spare parts storage'. Any aircraft repairable were done so and lived once again to fly another day. Even enemy aircraft were dismantled and stripped of all aluminium which was sent to the smelter, then to a factory where it was turned back either into new parts or into sheet metal. The results was that British aircraft were flying back over Germany with materials that were once Messerschmitts, Dorniers or Heinkels.

Assembly of Spitfires, Castle Bromwich Aero Factory.

Women workers sealing the fabric covering of petrol tanks at the Castle Bromwich factory, c.1943.

The number of new aircraft produced under Lord Beaverbrook did not always come up to the figures planned for. July 1940 was the only month that production exceeded the number planned. But under the circumstances, he did manage to provide enough so as to keep Fighter Commands 'head above water'.

Large scale plans were laid during 1937 for the construction by the Nuffield Group of a large new shadow factory at Castle Bromwich near Birmingham for Spitfire production. On April 21st, 1938, a contract was placed for 1000 Spitfires to be built at this new factory, of which actual construction had not then even begun.

By the time of the Munich crisis on 12-13 September 1938, only five Spitfires had been completed. In a following year, on April 29 further contracts were placed with Supermarine for 200 Spitfires, and on August 9 for 450. When Britain went to war on September 3rd, 1939, a total of 2160 Spitfires were already on order.

MONTHLY OUTPUT OF FIGHTER AIRCRAFT
JUNE - OCTOBER 1940

Month	Planned	Actual	Difference
June	1,164	1,163	-1
July	1,061	1,110	+49
August	1,143	1,087	-56
September	1,195	908	-287
October	1,218	917	-301

AIRCRAFT AVAILABLE FOR OPERATIONS

Month	Day	Total Aircraft Available
June	22	565
	29	587
July	6	644
	13	666
	20	658
	27	651
August	3	708
	10	749
	17	704
	24	758
	31	764
September	7	746
	14	725
	21	715
	28	732
October	5	734
	12	735
	19	734
	26	747
November	2	721

BRITISH WEEKLY FIGHTER AIRCRAFT PRODUCTION, APR-OCT 1940

Week Ending	Beaufighter	Defiant	Hurricane	Spitfire
6 Apr	0	5	35	14
13 Apr	1	3	38	17
20 Apr	0	3	41	13
27 Apr	0	6	40	14
4 May	0	3	34	15
11 May	0	5	41	12
18 May	0	4	40	14
25 May	0	4	59	17
1 Jun	0	8	87	22
8 Jun	0	2	79	22
15 Jun	0	7	67	25
22 Jun	2	8	75	21
29 Jun	0	13	68	26
6 Jul	0	12	65	32
13 Jul	0	12	57	30
20 Jul	1	11	67	41
27 Jul	4	14	65	37
3 Aug	3	13	68	41
10 Aug	5	10	64	37
17 Aug	5	11	43	31
24 Aug	5	8	64	44
31 Aug	5	3	54	37
7 Sep	5	11	54	36
14 Sep	6	10	56	38
21 Sep	4	6	57	40
28 Sep	0	10	58	34
5 Oct	0	12	60	32
12 Oct	4	11	55	31
19 Oct	6	8	55	25
26 Oct	9	16	69	42
2 Nov	3	10	56	41

- CHAPTER 6 -
A DAY IN THE LIFE OF
A BATTLE OF BRITAIN PILOT

I WOKE as the airman orderly tapped my shoulder and repeated, "Come along Sir, come along Sir, 4.30" in my ear. It was very cold in the hut and dark, so I wrestled with myself for a few minutes and then jumped out of bed and put on my flying kit quickly. Irvin trousers over my pyjamas, sweater, flying boots, scarf, Irvin jacket... I left the hut to look at my aeroplane.

I climbed into the cockpit out of which the fitter had just stepped, "Morning Williams, morning French, put my 'chute on the tail please," I checked the instruments one by one: petrol tanks full; tail trimming wheels neutral; airscrew fine pitch; directional; gyro set; helmet on reflector sight with oxygen and R/T leads connected - in fact everything as I liked it for a quick getaway when we scrambled.

Returning to the hut I found Hathaway, the orderly lighting the fire by the light of a hurricane lamp, while Chips lay fast asleep in a deck chair, his head lolling down on his yellow Mae-West. I lay down, and immediately became unconscious as if doped... What seemed the next moment I woke with a terrific start to see everyone pouring out of the hut... I could hear the telephone orderly repeating: "Dover 26,000; fifty plus bandits approaching from south-east."

Horton shouted, "Scramble Bill, lazy bastard," and automatically I ran out. Parachute on, pulled into cockpit by crew who had already started the engine. Straps, helmet, gloves, check the knobs, taxi out, get into the right position in my section and take off. I put the R/T on, and only then do I wake up and realize I am in the air flying with the distance between the ground and the Spitfire increasing all the time.

George Barclay 249 Sqn - Len Deighton/ Battle of Britain p122

As the twelve Spitfires manoeuvred into formation, and climbed for the east, I glanced down at my watch. Under ninety seconds. 'Not bad. Hope the old man was impressed.'

I started to wonder if we'd be too late again. Somehow the Controllers seemed slower these days. (They were - the communications network had been hard hit. But what they gave was far more accurate... well, sometimes. Everyone was learning.) "Parlor Leader, hullo, Parlor Leader. Many bandits approaching Dungeness, Angels 15 and above. Buster!"

Thin trails of smoke reached back from the exhaust ports. I looked over at my number two, "pull in Chips, pull in, your too far out... and pull up a bit... and watch that sun, that's where the bastards will be coming from", and from Chips, I wouldn't expect anything else for a reply, "and I suppose you want me to watch me mirror too sir!!!"

I had to start thinking tactics, we should really add a couple of thousand feet to our directed height, better to be a little too high, than caught in the murderous fire raining down from the 109s... Johnson, rehearsing in his mind his first - and only kill; a bomber nearly two weeks ago. Had it been a fluke? Could he ever do it again? Chips, with five to his credit, wondering if was really true that you got the DFM for six kills... he switched on the reflector sight, and turned the knurled knob until the brightness was exactly right. By now, a hardened veteran at 21, he knew what to expect. We were climbing higher; he set the bars to the wingspan of a 109. Chalkie Turner, on his first operational sortie, checking every dial, every setting again and again, practicing lifesaving tips he'd managed to pick up from the others. Get the head moving - check above, behind, to the beam... And Horton, humming contentedly away in his cockpit again, adrenaline pumping already, senses alive.

"Jesus Christ, it's the whole of the *Luftwaffe*..." Shimmering in the morning sun, wave upon wave of bombers, driving for London. Stepped above and behind, the serried ranks of Messerschmitts.

Battle of Britain London contrails

Covering mile upon mile of sky, as far as the eye could see. It was at once magnificent and terrible.

"Parlor Squadron, aim for the bombers. Look out for snappers coming down... here they come... Parlor, break, break."

Suddenly the sky was dissolved into whirling confusion, the headphones filled with snatches of command, of exultation, of warning, of stark terror.

"He's a flamer... Jeez, that was close... Hey, look out!"

"Go for the bombers... more at two o'clock..."

"Hold on Hamish, I'm coming. Hold on!"

Chips was jinking left, then right, as the tracer flashed past; suddenly, a twin reared up in his sights - long glasshouse, a 110. He let fly, saw little chips float off as the Messerschmitt completed its bunt. One damaged. He dived for the protection of the haze.

I was there again, and cautiously lifted the Spitfire up again, and was once again shocked by the sight of hundreds of black-crossed aircraft in unbroken phalanxes boring for London. What had all the sweat, the turmoil, the sacrifices of the last few minutes been for I wondered. I squirted at a Heinkel, and sank below the haze as it flew solidly on. I headed east, then rose again, hoping to come on the flank of the raid. Still they were there in dozens. By now, I was quite alone, fuel was low and circled long enough to take in the sight of bombs raining down over the docks. Fires springing up from Tilbury, a vast white splash in the Thames Estuary. Hope it's not one of one of our boys, I thought. I swung for home and three 109s suddenly appeared and slanted across from the right. Instinctively, I fired at the nearest; it rolled onto its back and dived away. I couldn't hang around to watch the results, with the other two whipping round to attack. Yellow noses - did that really mean a crack unit? - The thought was fleeting. I fired - the guns clattered briefly, then stopped. Time to go. I shoved the nose down, twisted, jinked, aileron turned, and all the time the 109s clinged to my elusive Spitfire. These boys were really good. With the altimeter unwinding like a sweep second hand, I finally found sanctuary right down among the Slough balloon barrage, and threaded my way carefully to the west.

I landed the Spitfire back at the home base, and bumped my way across the grass towards the hangars, throwing the hood back and filled my lungs with fresh, clean English air. I came to a standstill, and the ground staff were immediately taken to task in refuelling and rearming. I jumped out onto the wing, then down to the ground, "Running on fumes now, are we Sir" said the sergeant bending down and looking at me from under the wing. "We both are," I replied pulling my helmet and goggles off and making my way over to 'the hut', "both of us are exhausted."

"That bad is it Sir." he said,

"… and its going to get worse, "I said walking away almost shouting, "the bastards are in London."

As I got near to the dispersal hut, I saw a lean figure hurriedly put his head out of the window, "B Flight, "Scramble!!!" he had hardly got all the words out of his mouth as five or six bodies that were lazily lounging around outside sprang to their feet and ran to their awaiting aircraft. If they're going where I think they're going, there going to be in for it. By the time I got inside, the place was deserted except for the despatch clerk and Horton who had already beaten me down. "Any of the others back?" I asked pouring a cup of tea from the urn.

We both walked outside and sat down in the now vacant deckchairs. "No, just me, I was back first for a change," he paused, "… mind you, if it wasn't for being low on juice, I would have gone to Margate… they tell me it's nice there at this time of year."

As we sat there, almost in a melancholy silence, the others came back one by one… Chips, Hamish, Turner, it seemed that we had all made it back, a little tired, a little weary and our thoughts were with the other flight that had gone out to take our place.

The rest that we had all looked forward to was short lived. I was just about to go and see 'the old man' when the telephone rang again, there was a short silence then "Everybody up… scramble."

There had been hardly enough time to service the aircraft, but we ran all the same, fired up the Merlins and within seconds we were bouncing across the grass with throttles open, and doing it all over again.

The raid on London must be continuing as we were vectored to the same position we had been earlier. Again I started to think tactics, height, gain the advantage of height and again ascended two thousand more than our directed height.

With South London below, I caught a glimpse of a formation of enemy bombers as we turn southwest of London. I decide to manoeuvre our section to engage a group of Dornier Do17s from the beam but at the last instant the Germans turned so that a co-ordinated assault becomes impossible. My plan has gone astray, "Parlor Squadron, Parlor Squadron, okay boys… pick your target, break… break… break", I instruct the men to break up and make individual attacks, I took the leading Dornier. I turned, then closed fast, I fire a four second burst before diving underneath and swinging around for a second attack from the other side. This

A Royal Air Force Supermarine Spitfire trails smoke after attacking a German Heinkel He 111H/P bomber during the Battle of Britain.

time I fired for two seconds before banking away. The leading Dornier seems undamaged but suddenly the second bomber in the formation breaks away and falls into a dive. I turn off, and spot a single Messerschmitt Bf109 below and ahead. I follow it through the thick smoke billowing over the Thames and finally catch up with it over the Estuary. I fired for three seconds. The 109 is hit and a stream of black smoke trails behind his tail so I close in to 50 yards and fired for the last time. Pieces of the German fighter are torn away before it suddenly bursts into flames and then explodes in fire and brimstone with pieces of wreckage going in all directions.

I returned back towards London. The scene below is devastating. A huge spiralling cylinder of thick black smoke from burning warehouses near the docks billows steadily up into the clouds. The docks and warehouses are ablaze as London's East End is hammered.

The sun glints on the wings of the German bombers as they turn followed by the flak. Smaller planes dart in and out of the enemy formation, and the German planes are scattered but there are so many that they seem impossible to stop.

I make contact with Horton and Chips, we gain height where the air is a little clearer and more room to move in safety as the bombers are below us and with no sign of 109s. A short conversation and I instruct them to go in again. Horton picked a target and banked away and I lost sight of him as he went down. Chips put his nose down and headed for a group of three Dorniers, I follow him to the left and behind. "Parlor break, Parlor break, bandits two o'clock" I gathered that it would only be a matter of minutes before the 109s would be on us.

Chips is still diving down at the bombers. He is ahead of me as he closes in on a straggling Dornier. I continue to follow him down and saw him make a quarter attack on the German bomber. Large pieces fly off the enemy machine, then a wing crumples as it goes down spinning. An instant later I see a Spitfire which I assume to be that of Chips, spinning down with about a third of its wing broken off… Has there been a collision? The Spitfire spins wildly and he has no chance to bail out. Another casualty of this wretched war.

After doing my best to forget for the time being what I saw, taking time out to wallow in my feelings for Chips could spell trouble, one does not do that sort of thing and become another target for the enemy. I turned and attacked the bombers, evaded more 109s, I get a Dornier, and a probable, and possibly a share of a 109, but with ammunition exhausted, and fuel tanks close to empty, we land back at our airfield in ones and twos. Pilots climb wearily out of their cockpits in grim silence carrying in their minds an unforgettable picture of the seemingly impregnable bulk of the German formations and of the terrible firestorm in London.

For the front line squadrons, the daily routine varied little. Dowding had implied that each squadron be allowed one days rest a week, but this was not always possible. A normal battle day with a day fighter squadron could begin as early as 3.30am and carried on until stand down at around 8.00pm. Some flights or entire squadrons would be at readiness to take off within five minutes which, in actual practice, meant two or three minutes. Sometimes there would be a section on standby, with the pilots in their cockpits and able to be off the ground in a minute or so. Breakfast or a sandwich lunch would probably be brought to the dispersal points around the airfield.

It was now just after midday, we had flown two sorties today and that had taken the stuffing out of most of us, we were glad of the rest, no doubt other squadrons had been sent in to relieve us were over London, and we were now enjoying the rest, no matter how brief it may be. In the intervals between flights, we dozed on beds or chairs in the crew huts - or in tents for those at satellite airfields - or even on the grass. Some read, some played cards, draughts or chess. Tiredness inhibited conversation.

Periodically the telephone rang jerking us all into boggled eyed alertness. More often than not the telephone orderly would call one of us to some innocuous administrative call and the tension of another anticipated order to combat receded. That telephone played hell with our nerves. I don't think any of us pilots ever again appreciated the virtues of Mr. Bell's invention. Sooner or later though, the action charged instruction came through. The orderly would pause, listen and then bawl "Squadron scramble, Maidstone, Angels two zero."

Before he'd relayed the message we were away sprinting to our Spitfires, It was on again, the sheer hell of the mornings sorties were now behind us, as was the precious couple of hours rest that we had just enjoyed, only one thing remained in our thoughts, and that was to get to those Spitfires as quickly as possible.

As we ran, the fitters fired the starter cartridges and the propellers turned with engines roaring into life as flame and a puff of smoke was emitted from the Spitfires short exhausts. From strapping in to chocks away it was just a matter of seconds. We taxied to the take off point on the broad grass airfield, and pausing only to get the

British pilot Barrie Heath of No. 611 Squadron R.A.F. posing with his Spitfire fighter, 1940.

last aircraft to get into position, then stopping and looking towards the operations room waiting for the signal to take off. Seconds seem like minutes as we wait, "C'mon 'Matron' we haven't got all day" I said to which I got the curt reply, "Parlor Leader, you must learn to be a little patient!!" At last I led a flotilla of twelve Spitfires that were gunning their throttles and speeding away on the take-off in a wide vic formation of flights.

As we got airborne, we snapped the canopies shut, and pulling the undercarriage lever, the wheels were sucked into their wells. I glanced around on all sides making sure that the squadron were all in position. "Rastus Parlor airborne" I called over the R/T, to which the ground controller replied "OK, Parlor leader, one hundred plus bandits south of Ashford heading north west angels fifteen. Vector 130, Buster." Buster meant the fastest speed attainable, so there was no time for sightseeing this trip, Oh for a nice easy patrol!!

We struggled to gain every inch of height in the shortest possible time we gradually emerged out of the filthy black haze which perpetually hung like a blanket over London. Suddenly around 12,000 feet we broke through the smog layer and a different world emerged, startling in its sun drenched clarity. Long streaming contrails snaked way above us from the Channel coast as the Messerschmitt high flying fighters weaved protectively over their menacing bomber formations. Our radios became almost unintelligible as pilots in our numerous intercepting squadrons called out sightings, attack orders, warnings and frustrated oaths. Somehow, a familiar voice of any one of our pilots would call out and break through the radio chatter with an urgent "Parlor leader, bandits eleven o'clock level."

I fastened on to the tail of a yellow nosed Messerschmitt, I fought to bring my guns to bear as the range rapidly decreased, and when the wingspan of the enemy aircraft fitted snugly into the range scale bars of my reflector sight, I pressed the firing button. There was an immediate response from my eight Brownings which, to the accompaniment of a slight bucketing from my aircraft, spat a stream of lethal lead targetwards. 'Got you' I muttered to myself as the small dancing yellow flames of exploding 'De Wilde' bullets splattered along the Messerschmitts fuselage. Before I could fire another burst, two 109s wheeled in behind me. I broke hard into attack pulling the Spitfire into a climbing, spiralling turn, as I did so: a manoeuvre I had discovered in previous combats with 109s to be particularly effective. And it was no less effective now, the Messerschmitts literally "fell out of the sky" as they stalled in an attempt to follow me.

I soon found another target. About 3,000 yards in front of me, and at the same level, a Hun was just completing a turn preparatory to re-entering the fray. He must have seen me almost immediately, he rolled out of his turn towards me so that a head on attack became inevitable. Using both hands on the control column to steady the aircraft and to keep my aim steady, I peered through the reflector sight at the rapidly closing 109. We appeared to open fire together, and immediately a hail of lead thudded into my Spitfire. One moment, the Messerschmitt was a clearly defined shape, its wingspan nicely enclosed within the circle of my reflector sight, and the next it was on top of me, a terrifying blur which blotted out the sky ahead. Then we hit, his tailplane had dug into the Spitfires fuselage just behind the canopy, what damage had been done I didn't know, but the sound of ripping fuselage gave me real cause for concern.

The impact pitched me violently forward on to my cockpit harness, the straps of which bit viciously into my shoulders. At the same moment, the control column was snatched abruptly from my gripping fingers by a momentary, but powerful, reversal of elevator load. In a flash it was all over: there was clear sky ahead of me, and I thought for a moment, "God, I'm still alive," But I could see puffs of smoke and the odd flame coming from the engine cowling,the engine began to vibrate, slowly at first, but now, with increasing momentum causing the now regained control column to jump backwards and forwards in my hand. The bugger must have managed to get in a few shots whit found their target somewhere in the engine bay. I had to think quick, I closed the throttle, and reached forward and flicked off the ignition switches, but before I could do so, the engine seized and the airscrew came to an abrupt halt. I saw with amazement, that the blades had been bent almost double with the impact of the collision, the 109. How close was that I thought?

Smoke started to pour into the cockpit, I tugged at the hood release toggle, but could not release it, how I would welcome a rush of air now, I tried again with the normal release catch, but to no avail. There was only one thing to do, and that was to keep the aircraft under control. The speed had now dropped off considerably and with a strong backward pressure on the stick, I was able to keep a reasonable gliding altitude.

Frantically, I peered through the smoke and flame that was now enveloping the engine, trying to seek out what lay ahead. I daren't turn the aircraft, I had no idea as to what other damage may have

An Observer Corps spotter scans the skies of London.

been done, and at low level, even a small turn would be out of the question.

Through a miasmatic cloud of flame and smoke the ground suddenly appeared ahead of me. The next moment a post flashed by my wing tip and then the Spitfire struck the ground and ricocheted back into the air again finally returning to earth with a jarring impact, and once again I was jerked forward on to my harness. The straps held fast, and continued to do so as the aircraft ploughed its way through a succession of posts before finally coming to rest on the edge of a cornfield. The now dense smoke blinded my eyes, and my throat felt raw, I tried to keep swallowing, but it was almost as if my tongue was being welded to the roof of my mouth. For the first time, I became frantic with fear, I tore at my harness release pin then battered at the perspex hood in an effort to escape from the cockpit which entombed me. Then at last, with a splintering crash the hood finally cracked open, thus I was able to scramble clear from the cockpit and in the safety of the surrounding field.

For a while I was completely disorientated, come to think of it, where was I, the field was relatively quiet, and peaceful, the sky was clear, but I could see the vapour trails in one direction, "that surely must be over London, no, wait, where did we make contact with the enemy, God I don't know... yes I do, Ashford," the sky was just one huge sheet of silken haze, but a very bright spot indicated to me the position of the sun and that was the direction of west as it was now late afternoon.

I relieved myself of my helmet, and unbuttoned my Alvin jacket and decided to walk leaving the burning plane in the empty field.

Well, for me, another day over. All I had to do was to get to the nearest airfield and I would soon be back at base. My story would be told, along with the many others that would be told that evening, maybe in the mess, maybe down at the local pub, all it wanted was for someone to come up with a suggestion. After a few beers, or a game of cards, maybe a letter to the folks at home may be written… yes I owe them a letter, oh, better write a letter to "Chip's" family… a task we all dread, then the events of the day will soon be a thing of the past, remembered just how I want to remember them, or how I describe them in my letters. Tonight, I will sleep like a baby, lost in another world perhaps, only to be interrupted by that all too familiar call…" Come along Sir, come along Sir, 4.30"

- C H A P T E R 7 -

SPITFIRE IX, XI & XVI PILOTS NOTES

PART I - DESCRIPTIVE

Note - The numbers quoted in brackets after items in the text refer to key numbers of the illustrations in Part V.

INTRODUCTION

1.

i. The variants of the Spitfire IX, XI and XVI are distinguished by prefix letters denoting the general operating altitude or role and the suffix letter (e) is used where •5-in. guns replace •303-in. guns. The aircraft are all essentially similar, but the following table shows the main features that give the various versions their distinguishing letters:
The capacities of the main tanks are as follows:
F IX Merlin 61, 63 or 63A; two 20-mm. and four •303-in. guns.
LF IX Merlin 66; two 20-mm. and four •303-in. guns.
LF IX (e) Merlin 66; two 20-mm. and two 5-in. guns.
HF IX Merlin 70; two 20-mm. and four •303-in.
HF IX (e) Merlin 70; two 20-mm. and two 5-in. guns.
PR XI Merlin 61, 63, 63A or 70.
F XVI Merlin 266; two 20-mm. and two 5-in. guns.

ii. Merlin 61 and 63 engines have S.U.float-type carburettors, but on Merlin 66, 70 and 266 engines these are replaced by Bendix-Stromberg injection carburettors.

iii. All these marks of aircraft are fitted with Rotol 4-bladed hydraulic propellers and on the majority of the aircraft the wing tips are clipped.

iv. Later Mk. IX and XVIs have "rear view" fuselages which incorporate "tear-drop" sliding hoods.

FUEL, OIL AND COOLANT SYSTEMS

2. Fuel tanks - Fuel is carried in two tanks mounted one above the other (the lower one is self- sealing) forward of the cockpit. The top tank feeds into the bottom tank and fuel is delivered to the carburettor, through a filter, by an engine-driven pump. On Merlin 61 and 63 engine installations there is a fuel cooler, while on Bendix-Stromberg carburettor installations a de- aerator in the carburettor, for separating accumulated air from the fuel, is vented to the top tank. Later Mk. IX and all F. Mk. XVI aircraft mount two additional fuel tanks with a combined capacity of 75 gallons (66 gallons in aircraft with "rear view" fuselages); they are fitted in the fuselage behind the cockpit. These tanks should only be filled for special operations at the discretion of the appropriate Area Commander and normally their cocks should be wired OFF. If fitted in aircraft with "rear view" fuselages, they must not be used in any circumstances.

The capacity of the main tanks is as follows:

Top tank	48 gallons
Bottom tank	37 gallons or 47* gallons
Total	85 gallons or 95* gallons

* On some aircraft; generally those which have "rear view" fuselages.

An auxiliary "blister" drop tank of 30, 45 or 90 gallons capacity (on the PR XI, of 170 gallons capacity) can be fitted under the fuselage; the fuel from these tanks feeds the engine direct and docs not replenish the main tanks. To meet the possibility of engine cutting due to fuel boiling in warm weather at high altitudes, the main tanks arc pressurised; pressurising, however, impairs the self-sealing properties of the tanks and should, therefore, be turned OFF if a tank is holed.

3. Fuel cocks - The cock control for the main tanks is a lever (47) fitted below the engine starting pushbuttons and the pressurising control (50) is below the right-hand side of the instrument panel. The cock control (58) and jettison lever (59) for the auxiliary drop tank arc mounted together on the right-hand side of the cockpit, below the undercarriage control unit. The jettison lever is pulled up to jettison the drop tank, but cannot be operated until the cock control is moved forward to the OFF position. The cock for the rear fuselage tanks (when fitted) is to the left of the scat.

of the port wing and oil pressure (20) and temperature (17) gauges arc fitted on the instrument panel. When carrying an auxiliary drop tank of 170 gallons capacity a larger oil tank of either 8.5 or 14.5 gallons capacity must be fitted.

4. Fuel pumps - On Bendix-Stromberg carburettor installations an electric booster pump, operated by a switch on the left-hand side of the cockpit, is fitted in the lower main tank. On early aircraft this pump is not fitted, but a hand wobble pump is provided instead, just forward of the remote contactor.

Note - On aircraft which have rear fuselage tanks a second pump is fitted (in the lower rear tank) and the control switch described above then has three positions.

5. Fuel contents gauges and pressure warning light - The contents gauge (19) on the right-hand side of the instrument panel indicates the quantity of fuel in the lower main tank when the adjacent pushbutton is depressed. On aircraft with rear fuselage tanks a gauge (for the lower rear tank only) is mounted beside the main tanks' gauge. This also operates when the main tanks' gauge pushbutton is depressed. On later L.F. Mk. XVI aircraft the two gauges are mounted together, the left-hand dial (which is calibrated only up to 50 gallons) indicating the contents of the main tanks.

The fuel pressure warning light (18) is operative when the switch (34) on the throttle quadrant is on and comes on at any time when fuel pressure at the carburettor falls appreciably below normal.

6. Oil system - Oil is supplied by a tank of 75 gallons oil capacity under the engine mounting, which is pressurised to 2 1/2 lb./sq.in., and passes through a filter before entering the engine. An oil cooler is fitted in the underside

7. Engine coolant system.- On early aircraft only, circulation of the coolant through the underwing radiators is thermostatically controlled, the radiators being by-passed until the coolant reaches a certain temperature. The header tank is mounted above the reduction gear casing and is fitted with a relief valve. On all aircraft the radiator flaps are fully automatic and are designed to open at a coolant temperature of 115°C. A pushbutton is fitted on the electrical panel for ground testing; and there is a coolant temperature gauge (16) on the instrument panel.

8. Intercooler system.- On all aircraft the high temperatures resulting from two-stage supercharging necessitate the introduction of an intercooler between the supercharger delivery and the induction manifolds, particularly when S (high) gear is used. An auxiliary pump passes the coolant from a separate header tank to a radiator under the starboard wing, and thence through the supercharger casing to the intercooler, where the charge is cooled by loss of heat passing to the coolant. On early aircraft a thermostatically operated switch in the induction pipe is connected to the supercharger operating ram and causes it to change the supercharger to M (low) gear in the event of the charge temperature becoming excessive. This change of gear ratio is indicated to the pilot by a pushbutton, which springs out on the instrument panel. The supercharger will change back to high gear after the temperature of the charge has returned to normal and the pushbutton has been pushed in. If, however, the excessive temperature is of a permanent nature, due to failure of the intercoolcr system, the pushbutton will continue to spring out and the flight should be continued in low gear.

MAIN SERVICES

9. Hydraulic system - Oil is carried in a reservoir on the fireproof bulkhead and passes through a filter to an engine- driven pump for operation of the undercarriage.

10. Electrical system - A 12-volt generator supplies an accumulator which in turn supplies the whole of the electrical installation. A voltmeter (10) across the accumulator is fitted at the top of the instrument panel and a red light (40), on the electrical panel, marked POWER FAILURE, is illuminated when the generator is not delivering current to the accumulator.

    Note - If the electrical system fails or is damaged, the supercharger will be fixed in low gear and the radiator flaps will remain closed.

11. Pneumatic system - An engine-driven air compressor charges two storage cylinders to a pressure of 300lb./sq.in. for operation of the flaps, radiator flaps, supercharger ram, brakes and guns.

    Note - If the pneumatic system fails, the supercharger will be fixed in low gear, but the position of the radiator flaps will depend on the nature of the failure.

AIRCRAFT CONTROLS

12. Trimming tabs - The elevator trimming tabs are controlled by a handwheel (30) on the left-hand side of the cockpit, the indicator (24) being on the instrument panel. The rudder-trimming tab is controlled by a small hand-wheel (27) and is not provided with an indicator. The aircraft tends to turn to starboard when the handwheel is rotated clockwise.

13. Undercarriage control - The undercarriage selector lever (52) moves in a gated quadrant on the right-hand side of the cockpit.

    To raise the undercarriage the lever must be moved downwards and inwards to disengage it from the gate, and then moved forward smartly in one movement to the full extent of the quadrant. When the undercarriage is locked up the lever will automatically spring into the movement to the full extent of the quadrant. When the undercarriage is locked down the lever will spring into the rear gate.

Warning - The lever must never be moved into either gate by hand as this will cut off the hydraulic pressure.

An indicator in the quadrant shows DOWN, IDLE or UP depending on the position of' the hydraulic valve. UP and DOWN should show only during the corresponding operation of the undercarriage and IDLE when the lever is in either gate. If, when the engine is not running, the indicator shows DOWN, it should return to IDLE when the engine is started; if it does not, probable failure of the hydraulic pump is indicated.

14. Undercarriage indicators

    a. Electrical visual indicator. - The electrically operated visual indicator (2) has two semi-transparent windows on which the words UP on a red background and DOWN on a green background are lettered; the words are illuminated according to the position of the undercarriage. The switch (34) for the DOWN circuit is moved to the on position by a striker on the throttle lever as the throttle is opened.

    b. Mechanical position indicators. - On early aircraft a rod that extends through the top surface of the main plane is fitted to each undercarriage unit. When the wheels are down the rods protrude through the top of the main planes and when they arc up, the tops of the rods, which are painted red, arc flush with the main plane surfaces.

15. Undercarriage warning horn - The horn, fitted in early aircraft only, sounds when the throttle lever is nearly closed and the undercarriage is not lowered. It cannot be silenced until the throttle is opened again or the undercarriage is lowered. To lower the undercarriage the lever must be held forward for about two seconds, then pulled back in one

16. Flaps control - The split flaps have two positions only, up and fully down. They are controlled by a finger lever (5) on the instrument panel.

17. Wheel brakes - The brake lever is fitted on the control column spade grip and a catch for retaining it in the on position for parking is fitted below the lever pivot. A triple pressure gauge (25), showing the air pressures in the pneumatic system cylinders and at each brake, is mounted on the instrument panel.

18. Flying controls locking gear - Two struts are stowed on the right-hand "side of the cockpit aft of the seat. The longer strut and the arm attached to it lock the control column to the seat and to the starboard datum longeron, and the shorter strut, attached to the other strut by a cable, locks the rudder pedals. The controls should be locked with the seat in its highest position.

ENGINE CONTROLS

19. Throttle - The throttle lever (33) is gated at the climbing boost position. There is a friction adjuster (31) on the side of the quadrant. The mixture control is automatic and there is no pilot's control lever.

20. Propeller control
   i.   On early aircraft the speed control lever (35) on the inboard side of the throttle quadrant varies the governed r.p.m., from 3,000 down to 1,800.
   ii. On later aircraft the propeller speed control is interconnected with the throttle control. The inter-connection is effected by a lever, similar to the normal speed control lever, which is known as the override lever. When this is pulled back to the stop in the quadrant (the AUTOMATIC position) the r.p.m., are controlled by the positioning of the throttle lever. When pushed fully forward to the MAX. R.P.M., position it overrides the interconnection device and r.p.m., are then

governed at approximately 3,000. The override lever can be used in the same way as the conventional propeller speed control lever to enable the pilot to select higher r.p.m., than those given by the interconnection. It must be remembered that the interconnection is effected only when the override lever is pulled back to the stop in the quadrant; indiscriminate use of the lever in any position forward of this stop will increase fuel consumption considerably.

At low altitudes (and at altitudes just above that at which high gear is automatically engaged) the corresponding r.p.m., for a given boost with the override lever set to AUTOMATIC are as follows:

Boost (lb/.sq.in.)	R.P.M.
Below +3	1,800-1,850
At +7	2,270-2,370
At +12 (at the gate)	2,800-2,900
At +18 (throttle fully open)	3,000-3,050

   iii. A friction damping control (46) is fitted on the inboard side of the throttle quadrant.

21. Supercharger controls - The two-speed two-stage supercharger automatically changes to high gear at about 21,000 feet (14,000 feet on Merlin 66 and 11,000 feet on Merlin 266 installations) on the climb and back to low gear at about 19,000 feet (12,500 feet on Merlin 66 and 10,000 feet on Merlin 266 installations) on the descent. An override switch is fitted on the instrument panel by means of which low gear may be selected at any height. There is a pushbutton (42) on the electrical panel for testing the gear change on the ground, and a red light (13) on the instrument panel comes on when high-gear is engaged, on the ground or in flight.

22. Intercooler protector - Sec para. 8 and note. On early aircraft, should excessive charge temperatures cause the pushbutton (15) to spring out, it may be reset manually to allow the supercharger to return to high gear; it will, however, only remain in if the charge temperature has returned to normal.

23. Radiator flap control - The radiator flaps are fully automatic and there is no manual control. A pushbutton (41) for testing the radiator flaps is on the electrical panel.

24. Slow-running cut-out (Merlin 61 and 63 installations only) - The control on the carburettor is operated by pulling the ring (37) below the left-hand side of the instrument panel.

25. Idle cut-off control (Merlin 66, 70 and 266 installations only) - The idle cut-off valve on Bendix-Stromberg carburettors is operated by moving the short lever on the throttle quadrant through the gate to the fully aft position. On early installations this lever is not fitted, but the cut-off valve is operated by the ring (37), which on other aircraft operates the slow- running cutout.

Note - The idle cut-off control must be in the fully aft position, or cut-off position, at all times when a booster pump is on and the engine is not running; otherwise, fuel will be injected into the supercharger at high pressure and there will be, in consequence, a serious risk of fire.

26. Carburettor air intake filter control.
On tropicalised aircraft the carburettor air intake filter controlon the left-hand side of the cockpit has two positions OPEN and CLOSED (NORMAL INTAKE and FILTER IN OPERATION on later aircraft). The CLOSED (or FILTER IN OPERATION) position must be used for all ground running, take-off and landing and when Hying in sandy or dust- laden conditions.

Note -
i.   In the air it may be necessary to reduce speed to 200 m.p.h. I.A.S. or less, before the filter control lever can be operated.
ii. The filter control lever must always be moved slowly.

27. Cylinder priming pump - A hand-operated pump (48) for priming the engine is fitted below the right-hand side of the instrument pane).

28. Ignition switches and starter buttons -The ignition switches (1) arc on the left-hand side of the instrument panel and the booster-coil (22) and the engine starter (21) pushbuttons immediately below it. Each pushbutton is covered by a safety shield.

29. Ground battery starting - The socket for starting from an external supply is mounted on the starboard engine bearer.

OTHER CONTROLS

30. Cockpit floor - The cockpit door is fitted with a two- position catch which allows it to be partly opened, thus preventing the sliding hood from coming forward in the event of a crash or forced landing. It will be found that the catch operates more easily when the aircraft is airborne than when on the ground.

    Note - On aircraft with "tear-drop" hoods, the two-position catch should not be used.

31. Sliding hood controls
  i. On later Mk. IX and XVI aircraft the "tear-drop "hood is opened and closed by a crank handle mounted on the right-hand cockpit wall, above the undercarriage selector lever. The handle must be pulled inwards before it can be rotated. The hood may be locked in any intermediate position by releasing the crank handle, engaging the locking ratchet.
  ii. From outside the cockpit the hood may be opened and closed by hand provided the pushbutton below the starboard hood rail is held depressed.
  iii. The hood may be jettisoned in emergency (see para. 59).

32. Signal discharger - The recognition device fires one of six cartridges out of the top of the rear fuselage when the handle (39) to the left of the pilot's seat is pulled upwards. On some aircraft a pre-selector control (38) is mounted above the operating handle.

PART II - HANDLING

33. Mangement of the fuel system

Note - Except for special operations as directed by the appropriate Area Commander, the rear fuselage tanks must not be used and their cocks should be wired OFF. On aircraft with "rear view "fuselages they must not be used.

i) *Without a drop tank*

Start the engine, warm up, taxi and take-off on the main tanks; then, at 2,000 ft., change to the rear fuselage tanks (turning off the main tanks cock after the change has been made) and drain them; then revert to the main tanks.

ii. *When fitted with a drop tank*

a. Without rear fuselage tanks: Start the engine, warm up, taxi and take-off on the main tanks; then at 2,000 ft. turn ON the drop tank and turn OFF the main tanks cock. When the fuel pressure warning light comes on, or the engine cuts, turn OFF the drop tank cock and reselect the main tanks.

b. With rear fuselage tanks: Start the engine, warm up, taxi and take-off on the main tanks; then, at 2,000 ft. change to the rear fuselage tanks and continue to use fuel from them until they contain only 30 gallons. Turn ON the drop tank (turning OFF the rear fuselage tanks cock when the change has been made) and drain it, then change back to the rear fuselage tanks and drain them. Revert to the main tanks.

Note -

i. When it is essential to use all the fuel from the drop tank its cock must be turned OFF and the throttle closed immediately the engine cuts; a fresh tank without delay. The booster pump in the newly selected tank should be switched ON, or the hand wobble pump operated, to assist the engine to pick up but in addition to this it may be necessary to windmill the engine at high r.p.m., to ensure an adequate fuel supply.

ii. (ii) Drop tanks should only be jettisoned if this is necessary operationally. If a drop tank is jettisoned before it is empty a fresh tank should be turned ON before the drop tank cock is turned OFF.

iii. (iii) At no time must the drop Unk cock and the rear fuselage tanks cock be on together or fuel from the rear fuselage tanks will drain into the drop tank since the connection from these tanks joins the drop tank connection below the non-return valve.

iv. (iv) The drop tank cock must always be off when the tank has been jettisoned or is empty, otherwise air may be drawn into the main fuel system thus causing engine cutting.

(iii) Use of the booster pump(s)

a. The main tanks booster pump should be switched ON for take-off and landing and at all times when these tanks are in use in flight.

b. The rear fuselage tanks booster pump should be switched ON at all times when changing to, or using fuel from, these tanks.

34. Preliminaries

i. Check that the undercarriage selector lever is down; switch on indicator and see that DOWN shows green.

ii. Check the contents of the fuel tanks. If fitted with auxiliary tank(s) check that corresponding cock(s) are OFF.

iii. Test the operation of the flying controls and adjust the rudder pedals for equal length.

iv. On aircraft with Bendix-Stromberg carburettors ensure that the idle cut-off control is in the fully aft position, or cut-off position (see para. 25), then check the operation of the booster pump(s) by sound.

35. Starting the engine and warming up

(Aircraft with Merlin 61 0r 63 engines)

i.   Set the fuel cock - ON

ii. Ignition switches - OFF

Throttle - 1/2 in.-1 in. open

Propeller speed control lever - Fully forward

Supercharger switch - AUTO. NORMAL POSITION

Carburettor air intake filter control - CLOSED or FILTER IN OPERATION (see para. 26)

iii. If an external priming connection is fitted, high volatility fuel (Stores rcf. 34A/III) should be used for priming at temperatures below freezing. Work the Ki-gass priming pump until the fuel reaches the priming nozzles; this may be judged by a sudden increase in resistance.

iv. Switch ON the ignition and press the starter and booster-coil buttons. Turning periods must not exceed 20 seconds, with a 30 seconds wait between each. Work the priming pump as rapidly and vigorously as possible while the engine is being turned; it should start after the following number of strokes if cold:

Air Temp (°C)	+30	+20	+10	0	-10	-20
Normal Fuel	3	4	7	12	-	-
High volatility fuel	-	-	-	4	8	18

v.   At temperatures below freezing it will probably be necessary to continue priming after the engine has fired and until it picks up on the carburettor.

vi. Release the starter button as soon as the engine starts, and as soon as the engine is running satisfactorily release the booster- coil button and screw down the priming pump.

vii. Open up slowly to 1,000 to 1,200 r.p.m., then warm up at this speed.

36. Starting the engine and warming up (Aircraft with Merlin 66, 70 or 266 engines)

i. Set the fuel cock - ON

ii. Ignition switches - OFF
Throttle - 1/2 in.-1 in. open
Propeller speed control lever - Fully forward
Supercharger switch - AUTO. NORMAL POSITION
Carburettor air intake filter control - CLOSED or FILTER IN OPERATION (see para. 26)

iii. Switch ON the main tanks booster pump for 30 seconds (or operate the hand wobble pump for that period) then switch it OFF and set the idle cut-off control forward to the RUN position.
Note - If the idle cut-off control is operated by the ring described in para. 25, this must be held out (i.e., in the cut-off position) while the booster pump is ON or the hand wobble pump is being used.

iv. An external priming connection is fitted and high volatility fuel (Stores Ref. 34A/111) should be used for priming at temperatures below freezing. Operate the priming pump until fuel reaches the priming nozzles (this may be judged by a sudden increase in resistance to the plunger) then prime the engine (if Air temperature °C. it is cold) with the following number of strokes if cold:

Air Temp (°C)	+30	+20	+10	0	-10	-20
Normal Fuel	3	4	7	12	-	-
High volatility fuel	-	-	-	4	8	18

v. Switch ON the ignition and press the starter and booster-coil pushbuttons.

vi. When the engine fires release the starter button; keep the booster-coil button depressed and operate the priming pump (if required) .until the engine is running smoothly.

vii. Screw down the priming pump then open up gradually to 1,000-1,200 r.p.m., and warm up at this speed

viii. Check that the fuel pressure warning light does not come on then switch ON the main tanks booster pump (if fitted).

37. Testing the engine and services while warming up

i.   Check all temperatures and pressures and the operation of the flaps.

ii.   Press the radiator flaps test pushbutton and have the ground crew check that the flaps open.

iii. Test each magneto in turn as a precautionary check before increasing power further.

iv.   If a drop tank is carried check the flow of fuel from it by running on it for at least one minute.

After warming up to at least 15°C. (oil temperature) and 60°C. (coolant temperature),

v.   Open up to o lb./sq.in. boost and exercise and check the operation of the two-speed two-stage supercharger by pressing in and holding the test pushbutton. Boost should rise slightly and the red warning light should come on when high gear is engaged. Release the pushbutton after 30 seconds.

vi.   At the same boost, exercise (at least twice) and check the operation of the constant speed propeller by moving the speed control lever over its full governing range. Return the lever fully forward. Check that the generator is charging the accumulator by noting that the power failure warning light is out.

vii. Test each magneto in turn; if the single ignition drop exceeds 150 r.p.m., the ignition should be checked at higher power - sec sub. para, (ix) below.

Note - The following additional checks should be carried out after repair, inspection other than daily, when the single ignition drop at o lb/.sq.in.. boost exceeds 150 r.p.m., or at any time at the discretion of the pilot. When these checks are performed the tail of the aircraft must be securely lashed down.

viii. Open the throttle to the take-off setting and check boost and static r.p.m.

ix. Throttle back until r.p.m., fall just below the take-off figure (thus ensuring that the propeller is not constant speeding) then test each magneto in turn. If the single ignition drop exceeds 150 r.p.m., the aircraft should not be flown.

x. Where applicable (see para. 20) throttle back to +3 lb./sq.in. boost and set the override lever to AUTOMATIC; r.p.m., should fall to 1,800-1,850. Return the lever to MAX. R.P.M.

xi. Before taxiing check the brake pressure (80 lb./sq.in.) and the pneumatic supply pressure (220 lb./sq.in.).

38. Check list before take-off

Trimming tabs	At training load (full main tanks, no ammunition or external stores) 7,150 lb.	At normal full load (full main tanks, ammunition + 1x 45 gallon "blister" drop tank), 7,800 lb.	At max. load (full main and rear fuselage tanks, full ammunition, + 1 x 90 gallon "blister" drop tank) 8,700 lb.
Elevator	1 div nose down	Neutral	1. div nose down
Rudder	Fully right	Fully right	Fully right

P - Propeller Control Speed control (or override) lever fully forward

F - Fuel

Main tanks cock - ON

Drop tank cock - OFF

Rear fuselage tanks cock - OFF

Main tanks booster pump - ON

F - Flaps UP

Supercharger Switch - AUTO NORMAL POSITION

Red light out

Carburettor air - CLOSED or FILTER IN

Intake filter control OPERATION

39. Take-off

i. At training and normal loads +7 lb./sq.in. to +9 lb./sq. in.

boost is sufficient for take-off. After take-off, however, boost should be increased (where applicable) to +12lb./ sq.in. to minimise the possibility of lead fouling of the sparking plugs.

ii. There is a tendency to swing to the left but this can easily be checked with the rudder.

iii. When the rear fuselage tanks are full the aircraft pitches on becoming airborne and it is recommended that the undercarriage should not be retracted, nor the sliding hood closed, until a height of at least 100 feet has been reached.

iv. After retracting the undercarriage it is essential to check that the red warning light comes on, since if the undercarriage fails to lock UP the airflow through the radiators and oil cooler will be much reduced and excessive temperatures will result.

 Note - It may be necessary to hold the undercarriage selector lever hard forward against the quadrant until the red warning light comes on.

v. If interconnected throttle and propeller controls are fitted move the override lever smoothly back to AUTOMATIC when comfortably airborne.

vi. After take-off some directional retrimming will be necessary.

vii. Unless operating in sandy or dust-laden conditions set the carburettor air intake filter control to OPEN (or NORMAL INTAKE) at 1,000 ft.

40. Climbing - At all loads the recommended climbing speed is 180 m.p.h. (155 kts) I.A.S. from sea level to operating height.
Note-

i. With the supercharger switch at AUTO, high gear is engaged automatically when the aircraft reaches a predetermined height (sec para. 21). This is the optimum height for the gear change if full combat power is being used, but if normal climbing power (2,850 r.p.m. + 12 lb./sq.in. boost) is being used the maximum rate of climb is obtained by delaying the gear change until the boost in low gear has fallen to +8lb./sq.in. This is achieved by leaving the supercharger switch at MS until the boost has fallen to this figure,

ii. Use of the air intake filter reduces the full throttle height considerably.

41. General flying

Stability:

a. At light load (no fuel in the rear fuselage tanks, no drop tank) stability around all axes is satisfactory and the aircraft is easy and pleasant to fly.

b. When the rear fuselage tanks are full there is a very marked reduction in longitudinal stability, the aircraft tightens in turns at all altitudes and, in this condition, is restricted to straight flying, and only gentle manoeuvres; accurate trimming Is not possible and instrument flying should be avoided whenever possible.

c. When a 90-gallon drop tank is carried in addition to full fuel in the rear fuselage tanks, the aircraft becomes extremely difficult and tiring to fly and in this condition is restricted to straight flying and only gentle manoeuvres at low altitudes.

d. On aircraft which have "rear view" fuselage there is a reduction in directional stability so that the application of yaw promotes marked changes of lateral and longitudinal trim. This characteristic is more pronounced at high altitudes.

e. When 90 (or 170) gallon drop tanks are carried on these aircraft, they are restricted to straight flying and gentle manoeuvres only.

Controls:

The elevator and rudder trimming tabs are powerful and sensitive and must always be used with care, particularly at high speed.

Changes of trim:

Undercarriage up	NOSE UP
Undercarriage down	NOSEDOWN
Flaps up	NOSE UP
Flaps down Strongly	NOSE DOWN

There are marked changes of directional trim with change of power and speed. These should be countered by accurate use of the rudder trimming tab control. The firing of salvos of R/P's promotes a nose-up change of trim: this change is most marked when the weapons are fired in level flight at about 300 m.p.h

Flying at reduced air speed in conditions of poor visibility:
Reduce speed to 160 m.p.h. (140 kts) I.A.S., lower the flaps and set the propeller speed control (or override) lever to give 2,650 r.p.m.; open the sliding hood. Speed may then be reduced to 140 m.p.h.

42. Stalling

i. The stalling speeds, engine "off", in m.p.h. (knots) I.A.S. are Aircraft without "rear-view" fuselages

	At training load (full main tanks, no ammunition or external stores) 7,150 lb.	At normal full load (full main tanks, full ammunition + 1 x 45-gallon "blister" drop tank) 7,800 lb.	At max. load (full main and rear fuselage tanks, full ammunition, + 1 x 90 gallon "blister" drop tank) 8,700 lb.
Undercarriage and flaps up	90 (78)	93 (80)	100 (86)
Undercarriage and flaps down	75-79 (65-69)	80(69)	84(72)

Aircraft with "rear-view" fuselages

	At training load (full main tanks, no ammunition or external stores) 7,150 lb.	At normal full load (full main tanks, full ammunition + 1 x 45-gallon "blister" drop tank) 7,800 lb.	At max. load (full main and rear fuselage tanks, full ammunition, + 1 x 90 gallon "blister" drop tank) 8,700 lb.
Undercarriage and flaps up	95 (83)	78 (80)	115-117 (100-102)
Undercarriage and flaps down	83-84 (65-69)	85(98)	95(83)

The speeds above apply to aircraft which have "clipped" wings. On aircraft with "full span" wings these speeds are reduced (at all loads by 3-6 m.p.h. (or kts) I.A.S.

ii. Warning of the approach of a stall is given by tail buffeting, the onset of which can be felt some 10 m.p.h. (9 kts) I.A.S. before the stall itself. At the stall both wing and the nose drop gently. Recovery is straightforward and easy.

If the control column is held back at the stall tail buffeting becomes very pronounced and the wing drop is more marked.

Note - On L.F Mk. XVI aircraft warning of the approach of a stall is not so clear; faint tail buffeting can be felt some 5 mph. before the stall occurs.

iii. When the rear fuselage tanks are full there is an increasing tendency for the nose to rise as the stall is approached. This self-stalling tendency must be checked by firm forward movement of the control column.

43. Spinning

i. Spinning is permitted, but the loss of height involved in recovery may be very great and the following limits are to be observed:

(a) Spins are not to be started below 10,000 feet.

(b) Recovery must be initiated before two turns are completed.

ii. A speed of 180 m.p.h. (156 kts) I.A.S. should be attained before starting to ease out of the resultant dive.

iii. Spinning is not permitted when fitted with a drop tank, when carrying a bomb load, or with any fuel in the rear fuselage tank.

44. Diving

i. (i) At training loads, the aircraft becomes increasingly tail heavy as speed is gained and should, therefore, be trimmed into the dive. The tendency to yaw to the right should be corrected by accurate use of the rudder trimming tab control.

ii. (ii) When carrying wing bombs the angle of dive must not exceed 60°; when carrying a fuselage bomb the angle of dive must not exceed 40°.

Note - Until the rear fuselage tanks contain less than 30 gallons of fuel the aircraft is restricted to straight flight and only gentle manoeuvres.

45. Aerobatics

i. Aerobatics are not permitted when carrying any external stores nor when the rear fuselage tanks contain more than 30 gallons of fuel, and are not recommended when the rear fuselage tanks contain any fuel.

ii. The following minimum speeds in m.p.h. (knots) I.A.S. are recommended: Loop - 300 (260); Roll - 240 (206); Half-roll off loop - 340 (295); Climbing roll - 300(260)

iii. Flick manoeuvres are not permitted.

46. Check list before landing

i. Reduce speed to 160 m.p.h. (138 kts) I.A.S., open the sliding hood and check:

U - Undercarriage - DOWN

P - Propeller control - Speed control (or over- ride) lever set to give 2,650 r.p.m. - fully for ward on the final approach
Supercharger - Red light out
Carburettor air intake filter control - CLOSED (or FILTER IN OPERATION)

F - Fuel - Main tanks cock - ON, Main tanks booster pump (if fitted)- ON

F -Flaps - DOWN

ii. Check brake pressure (80 lb./sq.in.) and pneumatic supply pressure (220 lb./sq.in.).

Note - The rate of undercarriage lowering is much reduced at low r.p.m.

47. Approach and Landing

i. The recommended final approach speeds in m.p.h (Knots) I.A.S are:

a) Aircraft without "rear-view" fuselages

	Engine assisted	Glide
Flaps down	95 (82)	105 (90)
Flaps up	105 (90)	110 (95)

b) Aircraft with "rear-view" fuselages

	Engine assisted	Glide
Flaps down	100 – 105 (86-90)	115-120 (100-104)
Flaps up	115 (100)	120 – 125 (104-108)

"These speeds at which the airfield boundary is crossed; the initial straight approach should, however, be made at a speed 20-25 mph (17-21 kts. I.A.S. above these figures.)

Note - The speeds at which the airfield have clipped "wings; on aircraft with "full span "wings they may be safely reduced by 5 m.p.h. (or kts) I.A.S.

ii. Should it be necessary in emergency to land with the rear fuselage tnks still containing all their fuel the final engine assisted approach speeds given in (i) above should be increased by 10-15 m.p.h. (9-13 kts) I.A.S. The tendency for the nose to rise of its own accord at the 'hold off' must be watched (see para.42 (iii)); the throttle should be closed only when contact with the ground is made.

iii. The aircraft is nose-heavy on the ground; the brakes, therefore, must be used carefully on landing.

48. Mislanding

i. At normal loads the aircraft will climb away easily with the undercarriage and flaps down and the use of full take-off power is unnecessary.

ii. Open the throttle steadily to give the required boost,

iii. Retract the undercarriage immediately.

iv. With the flaps down climb at about 140 m.p.h. I.A.S. (v)

v. Raise the flaps at 300ft. and retrim.

49. Beam Approach

Spitfire Mk. XVI, II "training" load	Preliminary Approach	Inner Marker on Q.D.R	Outer marker on Q.D.R	Inner marker on Q.D.M
Indicated height (ft.)	Down to 1000	1000	700-800	1501q
Action	-	Lower the flaps,	Lower the under carriage +	Throttle back slowly
Resultant change of trim	-	Nose down	Nose down	Slightly nose down
I.A.S m.p.h. (knots)	170 (146)	160(138)	130 (111)	110 (95)
R.P.M.	2650	2650	3.000*	3.000*
Boost (level flight)	-2	-2	-3	
Boost (-500 ft.mm.)	-3	-3	-4	
Boost (overshoot)	-	-	-	+7

Remarks	OVERSHOOT
Reduce speed to 160 m.p.h (138 kts)	Open the throttle to give +7lb./sq.in.boost.
I.A.S before lowering the under carriage.	Raise the undercarriage and climb at 130 m.p.h. (112kts) I.A.S.
* With the override lever at MAX. R.P.M., r.p.m. may be 3000-3050 (see para 20)	Raise the flaps at 300 ft. and retrim.
Altimeter error at take-off 50ft	
Altimeter error at touchdown 60ft	
Add 2 mbs. To Q-F.E to give zero reading at touchdown.	

50. After landing

i. *Before taxiing*

Raise the flaps and switch OFF the main tanks booster pump (if fitted).

ii. *On reaching dispersal*

(a) Open up to 0 lb./sq.in. boost and exercise the two-Speed two-stage supercharger once (see para 35(v)).

(b) Throttle back slowly to 800-900 r.p.m. and idle at this

speed for a few seconds then stop the engine by operating the slow running cut-out or idle-cut off control.

(c) When the propeller has stopped rotating switch OFF the ignition and all other electrical services.

(d) Turn OFF the Fuel.

iii. Oil dilution

The correct dilution periods are:

At air temperatures above 10°C   1 minute

At air temperatures below 10°C   2 minutes

PART III - OPERATING DATA

51. Engine data: Merlins 61, 63, 66, 70 and 266

i.   Fuel - 100 octane only.

ii.   Oil - See Sec A.P.1464/C.37.

iii. The principal engine limitations are as follows:

	R.P.M.	Boost lb.sq./in	Temp Coolant °C	Oil
Max take off to 1,000 ft.	3000	+18*	135	-
Max climbing 1 hour limit	2850	+9	125	90
Max. continuous	2650	+7	105	90
Combat 5 minutes limit	3000	+18t	135	105

The figure in brackets is permissible for short periods.

With interconnected controls there is a tolerance on " maximum" r.p.m.—see para. 20.

* +12 lb./sq.in. on Merlin 61 and 63 engines.

t +15 lb./sq.in. on Merlin 61 and 63 engines.

Oil pressure: Minimum in flight   30 lb./sq.in.

Minimum temp. °C. for take off:

     Coolant   60 °C

     Oil   15 °C

52. Flying limitations

i. Maximum speeds in m.p.h. (knots) I.A.S.

Diving (without external stores), corresponding to a Mach. No. of 85:

Between S.L. and 20,000	450 (385)
20,000 & 25,000	430 (370)
25,000 & 30,000	390 (335)
30,000 & 35,000	340 (292)
Above 35,000	310 (265)
Undercarriage down	160 (138)
Flaps down	160 (138)

Diving (with the following external stores):

(a) With 1 x 500 lb. AN/M 58 bomb, or 1 X 500 lb. AN/M 64 bomb, or 1 500lb.AN/M76bomb,or1 X65 nickel bomb Mk. ll - Below 20,000 ft.*-440 (378)

(b) With 1 X 500 lb. S.A.P. bomb or Smoke bomb Mk. I- Below 25,000 ft. *—400 (344)

(c) With 10 lb. practice bomb - Below 25,000 ft.* - 420 (360)

*Above these heights the limitations for the "clean" aircraft apply.

ii. Maximum weights in lbs. For

take-off and gentle manoeuvres only Mks. IX & XVI —8,700*

For landing (except in emergency) Mks. IX & XVI - 7,450

For take-off, all forms of flying and landing Mks. IX - 7,800

*At this weight take-off must be made only from a smooth hard runway.

iii. Flying restrictions

(a) Rear fuselage tanks may be used only with special authority and never on aircraft with " rear view" fuselages.

(b) Aerobatics and combat manoeuvres are not permitted when carrying any external stores (except the 30-gallon "blister "type drop tank) nor when the rear fuselage tanks contain more than 30 gallons of fuel (but sec para. 45).

(c) When a (90 or 170) gallon drop tank or a bomb load is carried the aircraft is restricted to straight flying and only gentle manoeuvres.

(d) When wing bombs are carried in addition to a drop tank or fuselage bomb, take-off must be made only from a smooth hard runway.

(e) When carried, the 90 (or 170) gallon drop tank must be jettisoned before any dive bombing is commenced.

(f) Angle of dive when releasing a bomb or bomb load must not exceed 60° for wing bombs of 40° for a fuselage bomb.

(g) Except in emergency the fuselage bomb or drop tank must be jettisoned before fitted landing with wing bombs operationally.

(h) Drop tanks should not be jettisoned unless necessary operationally. While jettisoning, the aircraft should be flown straight and level at a speed not greater than 300 m.p.h. l.A.S.

This is achieved by leaving the supercharger switch at MS until the boost has fallen to this figure.

53. Position error corrections

From	120	150	170	210	240	290	m.p.h.
To	150	170	210	40	290	350	I.A.S
Add	4	2	0				m.p.h. or
Subtract			0	2	4	6	kts.
From	106	130	147	180	208	250	Knots
To	130	147	180	208	250	300	I.A.S

Note - On those aircraft which do not have interconnected throttle and propeller controls the propeller speed control lever must be advanced to the maximum r.p.m., position before the throttle is opened fully.

54. Maximum performance

   i. Climbing

     (a) The speeds in m.p.h. (knots) for maximum rate of climb are:

Sea level to 26,000ft.   160 (140) I.A.S.
26,000ft. to 30,000ft.   150 (130)
30,000ft. to 33,000ft.   140 (122)
33,000ft. to 37,000ft.   130(112)
37,000ft. to 40,000ft.   120 (104)
Above 40,000 ft.   100 (95)

(b) With the supercharger switch at AUTO, high gear is engaged automatically when the aircraft reaches a predetermined height (see para. 21). This is the optimum height for the gear change if full combat power is being used, but if normal climbing power (2,850 r.p.m. +12 lb./sq.in. boost) is being used the maximum rate of climb is obtained by delaying the gear change until the boost in low gear has fallen to +8 Ib./sq.in.

(1) Except in emergency landings should not be attempted until the rear fuselage tanks contain less than 30 gallons of fuel. Should a landing be necessary when they contain a greater quantity of fuel the drop tank should be jettisoned.

ii. Combat

Set the supercharger switch to AUTO and open the throttle

55. Economical Flying -

i. Climbing

On aircraft not fitted with interconnected throttle and propeller controls.

(a) Set the supercharger switch to MS, the propeller speed control lever to give 2,650 r.p.m., and climb at the speeds given in para. 54 (i), opening the throttle progressively to maintain a boost pressure of +7 lb./sq.in.

(A) Set the supercharger switch to AUTO when the maximum obtainable boost in low gear is +3 lb./sq.in., throttling back to prevent overboosting as the change to high gear is made.

On aircraft not fitted with interconnected throttle and propeller controls

(a) Set the supercharger switch to MS. set the throttle to give +7 lb./sq.in. boost and climb at the speeds given in para. 54 (i).

(b) As height is gained the boost will fail and it will be necessary to advance the throttle progressively to restore it. The throttle must not, however, be advanced beyond a position at which r.p.m., rise to 2,650. Set the supercharger switch to AUTO when, at this throttle setting, the boost in low gear has fallen to +3 lb./sq.in.

Note - Climbing at the speeds given in para. 54 (i) will ensure greatest range, but for ease of control (especially at heavy loads and with the rear fuselage tanks full of fuel) a climbing speed of 180 m.p.h. (155 kts) I.A.S. from sea level to operating height is recommended. The loss of range will be only slight.

ii. Cruising

The recommended speed for maximum range is 170 m.p.h. (147 kts) I.A.S. if the aircraft is lightly loaded. At heavy loads, especially if the rear fuselage tanks are full this speed can be increased to 200 m.p.h. (172 kts) I.A.S. without incurring a serious loss of range.

On aircraft fitted with interconnected throttle and propeller controls.

(a) With the supercharger switch at MS fly at the maximum obtainable boost (not exceeding + 7 lb./sq.in.) and obtain the recommended speed by reducing r.p.m., as required.

Note -
i. r.p.m. should not be reduced below a minimum of 1,800. At low altitudes, therefore, it may be necessary to reduce boost or the recommended speed will be exceeded.
ii. As the boost falls at high altitudes it will not be possible to maintain the recommended speed in low gear, even at maximum continuous r.p.m., and full throttle. It will then

he necessary to set the supercharger switch to AUTO. Boost will thus be restored and it will be possible to reduce r.p.m., again (as outlined in (a) above).

iii. In both low and high gears r.p.m., which promote rough running should be avoided.

On aircraft fitted with interconnected throttle and propeller controls

Set the supercharger switch to MS and adjust the throttle to obtain the recommended speed. Avoid a throttle setting which promotes rough running.

Note - At moderate and high altitudes it will be necessary to advance the throttle progressively to restore the falling boost and thus maintain the recommended speed.

Now as the throttle is opened r.p.m., will increase and at a certain height the recommended speed will be unobtainable even at a throttle setting which gives 2,650 r.p.m.. At this height the supercharger switch should be set to AUTO and the throttle then adjusted as before to maintain the recommended speed.

56. Fuel capacities and consumption -

i. Normal fuel capacity:

Top tank	48 gallons
Bottom tank	37 gallons
Total	85 gallons

ii. Long-range fuel capacities:

With 30 gallon "blister" drop tank	115 gallons
With 45 gallon "blister" drop tank	130 gallons
With 90 gallon "blister" drop tank	175 gallons
With 170 gallon "blister" drop tank	255 gallons
With rear fuselage tanks:	
Early aircraft	160 gallons
Later aircraft	151 gallons

Note - On some aircraft these capacities increased by 10 gallons.

iii. Fuel consumptions:

The approximate fuel consumptions (gals./hr.) are as follows, weak mixture (as obtained at +7 lb./sq.in. boost and below): r.p.m.:

Boost lb./sq.in	2,650 r.p.m.	2,400	2,200	2,000	1,800
+7	80	-	-	-	-
+4	70	66	61	54	-
+2	66	61	57	50	43
0	60	55	51	45	39
-2	53	49	45	40	35
-4	45	42	38	34	30

Rich mixture (as obtained above -f 7 lb./sq.in. boost): Boost

Boost lb./sq.in	R.P.M.	gals./hr.
+15	3000	130
+12	2850	105

Note - The above approximate consumptions apply for all Marks of engine. Accurate figures giving the variation in consumption with height and as between low and high gear are not available.

PART IV - EMERGENCIES

57 Undercarriage emergency operation

i.   If the selector lever jams and cannot be moved to the fully down position after moving it out of the gate, return it to the fully forward position for a few seconds to take the weight of the wheels off the locking pins and allow them to turn freely, then move it to the DOWN position.

ii. If, however, the lever is jammed so that it cannot be moved either forward or downward, it can be released by taking the weight of the wheels off the locking pins either by pushing the control column forward sharply or inverting the aircraft. The lever can then be moved to the DOWN position.

iii. If the lever springs into the gate and the indicator shows that the undercarriage is not locked down, hold it fully down for a few seconds. If this is not successful, raise and then lower the undercarriage again.

iv. If the undercarriage still docs not lock down, ensure that the lever is in the DOWN position (this is essential) and push the emergency lever forward and downward through 1800.

Note -

(a) The emergency lever must not be returned to its original position and no attempt must be made to raise the undercarriage until the CO_2 cylinder has been replaced.

(b) If the CO_2 cylinder has been accidentally discharged with the selector lever in the up position, the undercarriage will not lower unless the pipeline from the cylinder is broken, either by hand or by means of the crowbar.

58. Failure of the pneumatic system

i. If the flaps fail to lower when the control is moved to the DOWN position, it is probably due to a leak in the pipeline, resulting in complete loss of air pressure and consequent brake failure.

ii. Alternatively, if a leak develops in the flaps control system the flaps will lower, but complete loss of air pressure will follow and the brakes will become inoperative. (In this case a hissing sound may be heard in the cockpit after selecting flaps DOWN.)

iii. In either case the flaps control should immediately be returned to the UP position in order to allow sufficient pressure to build up, so that a landing can be made with the brakes operative but without Haps.

Note - As a safeguard pilots should always check the pneumatic pressure supply after selecting flaps DOWN.

59. Hood jettisoning

The hood may be jettisoned in an emergency by pulling the rubber knob inside the top of the hood forward and downward and then pushing the lower edge of the hood outwards with the elbows.

Warning - Before jettisoning the hood the seat should be lowered and the head then kept well down.

60. Forced landing - In the event of engine failure necessitating a forced landing:

i. If a drop tank or bomb load is carried it should be jettisoned.

ii. The fuel cut-off control should be pulled fully back.

iii. The booster pump (if fitted) should be switched OFF.

iv. The sliding hood should be opened and the cockpit door set on the catch (see para. 51).

v. A speed of at least 150 m.p.h. (130 kts) I.A-S. should be maintained while manoeuvring with the undercarriage and flaps retracted.

vi. The flaps must not be lowered until it is certain that the selected landing area is within easy gliding reach.

vii. The final straight approach should be made at the speeds given in para. 47.

viii. If oil pressure is still available the glide can be lengthened considerably by pulling the propeller speed control (or override) lever fully back past the stop in the quadrant.

61. Ditching

i. Whenever possible the aircraft should be abandoned by parachute rather than ditched, since the ditching qualities arc known to be very poor.

ii. When ditching is inevitable any external stoics should be jettisoned (release will be more certain if the aircraft is gliding straight) and the following procedure observed:

(a) The cockpit hood should be jettisoned.

(b) The flaps should be lowered in order to reduce the touchdown speed as much as possible.

(c) The undercarriage should be kept retracted.

(d) The safety harness should be kept tightly adjusted and the R/T plug should be disconnected.

(e) The engine, if available, should be used to help make the touchdown in a taildown attitude at as low a forward speed as possible.

(f) Ditching should be along the swell, or into wind if the swell is not steep, but the pilot should be prepared for a tendency for the aircraft to dive when contact with the water is made.

62. Crowbar - A crowbar for use in emergency is stowed in spring clips on the cockpit door.

PART V - ILLUSTRATIONS

1 - Ignition switches, 2 - Undercarriage indicator, 3 - Oxygen regulator,
4 - Navigation lamps switch, 5 - Flap control, 6 - Instrument flying panel,
7 - Lifting ring for sunscreen, 8 - Reflector sight switch, 9 - Reflector sight
base, 10 - Voltmeter, 11 - Cockpit ventilator control,

INSTRUMENT PANEL

12 - Engine Speed indicator, 13 - Supercharger warning lamp, 14 - Boost
gauge, 15 - Intercooler protector pushbutton, 16 - Coolant temp gauge,
17 - Oil temp Gauge, 18 - Fuel Pressure warning lamp, 19 - Fuel contents
gauge, 20 - Oil Pressure gauge, 21 - Engine starter pushbutton, 22 -
Booster-Coil pushbutton, 23 - Cockpit floodlight switches, 24 - Elevator tap
position indicator, 25 - Brake tripe pressure gauge

26 - Crowbar, 27 - Rudder trimming tab hand wheel, 28 - Pressure head heater switch, 29 - Two position door catch lever, 30 - Elevator trimming tab hand-wheel, 31 - Throttle lever friction adjustor, 32 - Floodlight, 33 - Throttle lever, 34 - Undercarriage indicator master switch, 35 - Propeller speed control, 36 - T.R.1133 pushbutton control, 37 - Slow-running- cutout,

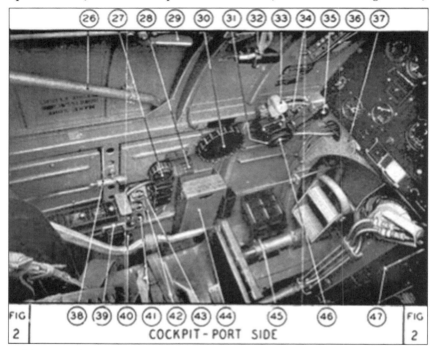

COCKPIT - PORT SIDE

38 - signal Discharger pre-selector control, 39 - Signal discharger firing control, 40 - Power Failure Lamp, 41 - Radiator ground test pushbutton, 42 - Supercharger ground test pushbutton, 43 - Oil dilution pushbutton, 44 - Map case, 45 - Rudder pedal adjusting star wheel, 46 - Propeller control friction adjuster, 47 - Fuel Cock control

48 - Engine priming pump, 49 - Signaling switchbox, 50 - Fuel tank pressure cock, 51 - Remote contactor and contactor switch, 52 - Undercarriage control lever, 53 - IFF pushbutton, 54 - Harness release control, 55 - IFF master switch, 56 - Undercarriage Control Lever

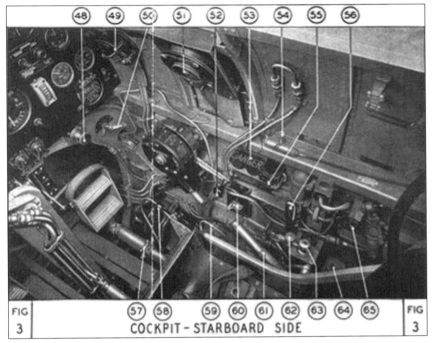

FIG 3 | COCKPIT - STARBOARD SIDE | FIG 3

57 - Rudder pedal adjusting star wheel, 58 - Drop rank cock control, 59 - Drop tank jettison lever, 60 - Windscreen de-icing cock, 61 - Seat Adjustment lever, 62 - Windscreen de-icing needle valve, 63 - Windscreen de-icing pump, 64 - Microphone/telephone socket, 65 - Oxygen supply cock

- C H A P T E R   8 -

JULY, 1940 AIR PUBLICATION 1565B PILOT'S NOTES

SECTION 1
PILOT'S CONTROLS AND EQUIPMENT

INTRODUCTION

The Spitfire IIA and IIB are single seat, low wing monoplane fighters each fitted with a Merlin XII engine and a de Havilland 20° (P.C.P.) or Rotol 35° constant speed airscrew.

MAIN SERVICES

2. Fuel system – Fuel is carried in two tanks mounted one above the other (the lower one is self-sealing) forward of the cockpit and is delivered by an engine driven pump. The tank capacities are as follows:

Top tank: 48 gallons
Bottom tank: 37 gallons

The top tank feeds into the lower tank, and the fuel cock controls, one for each tank, are fitted below the instrument panel.

3. Oil system - Oil is supplied by a tank of 5.8 gallons capacity fitted below the engine mounting, and two oil coolers in tandem are fitted in the underside of the port plane.

4. Hydraulic system - An engine-driven hydraulic pump supplies the power for operating the under-carriage.

5. Pneumatic system - An engine-driven air compressor feeds two storage cylinders for operation of the flaps, brakes, guns and landing lamps. The cylinders are connected in series, each holding air at 200 lb/sq. in pressure.

6. Electrical system - A 12 Volt generator, controlled by a switch above the instrument panel, supplies an accumulator which in turn supplies the whole of the electrical installation. There is a voltmeter on the left of the switch.

AEROPLANE CONTROLS

7.

    a. Primary flying controls and locking devices - The control column is of the spade-grip pattern and incorporates the brake lever and gun and cannon firing control. The rudder pedals have two positions for the feet and are adjustable for leg reach by rotation of star wheels on the sliding tubes.

    b. Control locking struts are stowed on the right hand side of the cockpit, behind the seat. To lock the control column, the longer strut should be clamped to the control column handle at one end and the other end inserted in a key-hole slot in the right hand side of the seat. The fixed pin on the free end of the arm attached to this strut at the control column end should then be inserted in a lug on the starboard datum longeron, thus forming a rigid triangle between the column, the seat and the longeron.

    c. To lock the rudder pedals, a short bar with a pin at each end is attached to the other struts by a cable. The longer of the two pins should be inserted in a hole in the starboard star wheel bearing and the shorter in an eyebolt on the fuselage frame directly below the front edge of the seat. The controls should be locked with the seat in its highest position.

8. Flying instruments - A standard blind flying instrument panel is incorporated in the main panel. The instruments comprise airspeed indicator, altimeter, directional gyro, artificial horizon, rate of climb and descent indicator, and turn and bank indicator.

9. Trimming tabs - The elevator trimming tabs are controlled by a hand wheel on the left hand side of the cockpit, the indicator being on the instrument panel. The rudder trimming tab is controlled by a small hand wheel and is not provided with an indicator. The aeroplane tends to turn to starboard when the handwheel is rotated clockwise.

10.

    a.   Undercarriage control and Indicators (visual and audible - The undercarriage selector lever moves in a gated quadrant, on the right hand side of the cockpit. An automatic cut-out in the control moves the selector lever into the gate when it has been pushed or pulled to the full extent of the quadrant.

    b.   To raise the undercarriage the lever is pushed forward, but it must first be pulled back and then across to disengage it from the gate. When the undercarriage is raised and locked, the lever will spring into the forward gate.

    c.   To lower the undercarriage the lever is pulled back, but it must be pushed forward and then across to disengage it from the gate. When the undercarriage is lowered and locked, the lever will spring into the rear gate.

    d.   Electrical visual indicator - The electrically operated visual indicator has two semi-transparent windows on which the words UP on a red background and DOWN on a green background are lettered; the words are Illuminated according to the position of the undercarriage. The switch for the DOWN circuit of the indicator is mounted on the inboard side of the throttle quadrant and is moved to the ON position by means of a striker on the throttle lever; this switch should be returned to the OFF position by hand when the aeroplane is left standing for any length of time. The UP circuit is not controlled by this switch.

    e.   Mechanical position indicator - A rod that extends through the top surface of the main plane is fitted to each undercarriage unit. When the wheels are down the rods protrude through the top of the main planes and when they are up the top of the rods, which are painted red, are flush with the main plane surfaces.

f. Warning horn - The push switch controlling the horn is mounted on the throttle quadrant and is operated by a striker on the throttle lever. The horn may be silenced, even though the wheels are retracted and the engine throttled back, by depressing the push button on the side of the throttle quadrant. As soon as the throttle is again advanced beyond about one quarter of its travel the push-button is automatically released and the horn will sound again on its return.

11. Flap control - The split flaps have two positions only, up and fully down. They cannot therefore, be used to assist take-off. They are operated pneumatically and are controlled by a finger lever: A flap indicator was fitted only on early Spitfire I aeroplanes.

12.

a. Undercarriage emergency operation - A sealed high-pressure cylinder containing carbon-dioxide and connected to the undercarriage operating jacks is provided for use in the event of failure of the hydraulic system. The cylinder is mounted on the right hand side of the cockpit and the seal can be punctured by means of a red painted lever beside it. The handle is marked EMERGENCY ONLY and provision is made for fitting a thin copper wire seal as a check against inadvertent use.

b. If the hydraulic system fails, the pilot should ensure that the undercarriage selector lever is in the DOWN position (this is essential) and push the emergency lowering lever forward and downward. The angular travel of the emergency lever is about 100° for puncturing the seal of the cylinder and then releasing the piercing plunger; it must be pushed through this movement and allowed to swing downwards. NO attempt should be made to return it to its original position until the cylinder is being replaced.

13. Wheel brakes - The control lever for the pneumatic brakes is fitted on the control column spade grip; differential control of the brakes is provided by a relay valve connected to the rudder bar. A catch for retaining the brake lever in the on position for parking is fitted below the lever pivot. A triple pressure gauge, showing the air pressures in the pneumatic system cylinders and at each brake, is mounted on the left hand side of the instrument panel.

ENGINE CONTROLS

14. Throttle and mixture controls - The throttle and mixture levers are fitted in a quadrant on the port side of the cockpit. A gate is provided for the throttle lever in the take-off position and an interlocking device between the levers prevents the engine from being run on an unsuitable mixture. Friction adjusters for the controls are provided on the side of the quadrant.

15. Automatic boost cut-out - The automatic boost control may be cut out by pushing forward the small red painted lever at the forward end of the throttle quadrant.

16. Airscrew controls - The control lever for the de Havilland 20° or Rotol 35° constant speed airscrew is on the throttle quadrant. The de Havilland 20° airscrew has a Positive Coarse Pitch position which is obtained in the extreme aft position of the control lever, when the airscrew blades are held at their maximum coarse pitch angles and the airscrew functions as a fixed airscrew.

17. Radiator flap control - The flap at the outlet end of the radiator duct is operated by a lever and ratchet on the left hand side of the cockpit. To open the flap, the lever should be pushed forward after releasing the ratchet by depressing the knob at the top of the lever'. The normal minimum drag position of the flap lever for level flight is shown by a red triangle on the top of the map case fitted beside the lever. A notch beyond the normal position in the aft direction provides a position of the lever when the warm air is diverted through ducts into the main planes for heating the guns at high altitude.

18. Slow-running cut-out - The control on the carburettor is operated by pulling the ring on the right hand side of the instrument panel.

19. Fuel cock controls and contents gauges - The fuel cock controls, one for each tank, are fitted at the bottom of the instrument panel. With the levers in the UP position the cocks are open. Either tank can be isolated, if necessary. The fuel contents gauge on the instrument panel indicates the contents of the lower tank, but only when the adjacent push button is pressed.

20. Fuel priming pump - A hand-operated pump for priming the engine is mounted below the right hand side of the instrument panel.

21. Ignition switches - The ignition switches are on the left hand bottom corner of the instrument panel.

22. Cartridge starter - The starter push-button at the bottom of the instrument panel operates the L.4 Coffman starter and the booster coil. The control for re loading the breech is below the right-hand side of the instrument panel and is operated by slowly pulling on the finger ring and then releasing it.

23. Hand starting - A starting handle is stowed behind the seat. A hole in the engine-cowling panel on the star board side gives access for connecting the handle to the hand starting gear.

24. Engine instruments - The engine instruments are grouped on the right hand side of the instrument panel and comprise the following: engine-speed indicator, fuel pressure gauge, boost gauge, oil pressure gauge, oil inlet temperature gauge, radiator outlet temperature gauge and fuel contents gauge.

COCKPIT ACCOMMODATION AND EQUIPMENT

25. Pilot's seat control - The seat is adjustable for height by means of a lever on the right hand, side of the seat.

26. Safety harness release - In order that the pilot may lean forward without unfastening his harness, a release catch is fitted to the right of the seat.

27. Cockpit door - To facilitate entry to the cockpit a portion of the coaming on the port side is hinged. The door catches are released by means of a handle at the forward end. Two position catches are incorporated to allow the door to be partly opened before taking off or landing in order to prevent the hood from sliding shut in the event of a mishap.

28. Hood locking control - The sliding hood is provided with spring catches for holding it either open or shut; the catches are released by two finger levers at the forward end of the hood. From outside, with the hood closed, the catches can be released by depressing a small knob at the top of the windscreen. Provision is made on the door to prevent the hood from sliding shut if the aeroplane over turns on landing.

29. Direct vision panel - A small knock-out panel is provided on the right hand side of the hood for use in the event of the windscreen becoming obscured.

30. Cockpit lighting - A floodlight is fitted on each side of the cockpit and is dimmed by a switch immediately below the instrument panel.

31. Cockpit heating and ventilation - A small adjustable flap on the starboard coaming above the instrument panel is provided for ventilation of the cockpit. The flap is opened by turning a knurled nut underneath the flap.

32. Oxygen - A standard regulator unit is fitted on the left hand side of the instrument panel and a bayonet socket is on the right hand side of the cockpit. A separate cock is provided in addition to the regulator.

33. Mirror - A mirror is fitted at the top of the windscreen.

34. Map cases - A metal case for a writing pad and another for maps, books, etc. are fitted on the left hand side or the cockpit. Stowage for a height-and-airspeed computer is provided below the wireless remote contactor.

OPERATIONAL EQUIPMENT AND CONTROLS

35.

a. Guns and cannon - The eight machine guns on the Spitfire IIA are fired pneumatically by a push-button on the control column spade grip. The compressed air supply is taken from the same source as the brake supply, the available pressure being shown by the gauge. The push- button is surrounded by a milled sleeve which can be rotated by a quarter of a turn to a safe position in which it prevents operation of the button. The SAFE and FIRE positions are engraved on the sleeve and can also be identified by touch as the sleeve has an indentation which is at the bottom when the sleeve is in the SAFE position and is at the side when the sleeve is turned to the FIRE position.

b. The guns and cannon on the Spitfire IIB are fired pneumatically by a triple push-button on the control column spade grip. A milled finger lever extending from the bottom of the push-button casing provides the means of locking the button in the SAFE position, SAFE and FIRE being engraved on the adjacent casing. When the lever is in the FIRE position a pip extends also from the top of the casing enabling the pilot to ascertain by feel the setting of the push-button.

c. To prevent accidental firing of the cannon on the ground, a safety valve is fitted in the firing system. This is mounted below the undercarriage control unit and is coupled to the undercarriage locking pin cable in such a way that the cannon firing system is inoperative when the wheels are locked down. For practice firing at the butts, however, a finger lever on the safety valve can be operated to allow the use of the firing system.

d. The cannon are cocked pneumatically by a cocking valve mounted on the right hand side of the cockpit.

36.

a. Reflector gun sight - For sighting the guns and cannon a reflector gun sight is mounted on a bracket above the instrument panel. A main switch and dimmer switch are fitted below the mounting bracket. The dimmer switch has three positions marked OFF, NIGHT and DAY. Three spare lamps for the sight are stowed in holders on the right hand side of the cockpit.

b. When the sight is used during the day the dimmer switch should be in the DAY position in order to give full illumination, and if the background of the target is very bright, a sun-screen can be slid behind the windscreen by pulling on the ring at the top of the instrument panel. For night use the dimmer switch should be in the NIGHT position; in this position a low-wattage lamp is brought into circuit and the light can be varied by rotating the switch knob.

37.

a. Camera - A G.42B cine-camera is fitted in the leading edge of the port plane, near the root end and is operated by the cannon-firing button on the control column spade grip, a succession of exposures being made during the whole time the button is depressed, provided the selector switch on the left hand side of the cockpit is ON.

b. A footage indicator and an aperture switch are mounted on the wedge plate above the throttle lever. The switch enables either of two camera apertures to be selected, the smaller aperture being used for sunny weather. A stowage clip is provided to receive the electrical cable when the indicator and switch are not fitted.

NAVIGATIONAL, SIGNALLING AND LIGHTING EQUIPMENT

38.

a. Wireless - The aeroplane is equipped with a combined transmitter-receiver, either type T.R.9D or T.R.H33, and an R.3OO2 set.

b. With the T.R.9D installation a Type C mechanical controller is fitted on the port side of the cockpit above the throttle lever and a remote contactor and contactor master switch are fitted on the right hand side of the cockpit. The master contactor is mounted behind the pilot's headrest and a switch controlling the heating element is fitted on the forward bracket of the mounting. The heating element should always be switched OFF when the pilot leaves the aeroplane. The microphone/telephone socket is fitted on the right hand side of the pilot's seat.

c. With the T.R.1133 installation the contactor gear and microphone/telephone socket are as for the T.R.9D installation, but the Type C mechanical controller is replaced by a push-button electrical control unit.

39.

a. Navigation and identification lamps - The switch controlling the navigation lamps is on the instrument panel.

b. The upward and downward identification lamps are controlled from the signalling switchbox on the right hand side of the cockpit. This switchbox has a switch for each lamp and a morsing key, and provides for steady illumination or morse signalling from each lamp or both. The switch lever has three positions: MORSE, OFF and STEADY.

c. The spring pressure on the morsing key can be adjusted by turning the small ring at the top left hand corner of the switchbox, adjustment being maintained by a latch engaging one of a number of notches in the ring. The range of movement of the key can be adjusted by opening the cover and adjusting the screw and locknut at the centre of the cover.

40. Landing lamps - The landing lamps, one on each side of the aeroplane, are housed in the undersurface of the main plane. They are lowered and raised by a finger lever below the instrument panel. Each lamp has an independent electrical circuit and is controlled by a switch above the pneumatic control lever with the switch in the central position both lamps are off; when the switch is moved to the left or to the right, the port or the star- board lamp respectively, is illuminated. A lever is provided to control the dipping of both landing lamps. On pulling up the lever the beam is dipped.

41. Signal discharge - A straight pull of the toggle control on the left hand side of the cockpit fires one of the cartridges out of the top of the fuselage, aft of the cockpit.

DE-ICING EQUIPMENT

42.

a. Windscreen de-icing - A tank containing the de-icing solution is mounted on the left hand side of the cockpit directly above the bottom longeron. A cock is mounted above the tank, and a pump and a needle valve to control the flow of the liquid are mounted below the undercarriage emergency lowering control. Liquid is pumped from the tank to a spray at the base of the windscreen, from which it is sprayed upwards over the front panel of the screen.

b. The flow of liquid is governed by the needle valve, after turning ON the cock and pushing down the pump plunger to its full extent. The plunger will return to the extended position on its own, and if required it can be pushed down again. When de-icing is no longer required the cock should be turned to the OFF position.

43. Pressure head heater switch - The heating element in the pressure head is controlled by switch below the trimming tab handwheels. It should be switched off on landing in order to conserve the battery.

EMERGENCY EQUIPMENT

44. Hood jettisoning - The hood may be jettisoned in an emergency by pulling the lever mounted inside the top of the hood in a forward and downward movement, and pushing the lower edge of the hood outboard with the elbows. On aeroplanes not fitted with a jettison type hood, a crowbar is provided to assist in jettisoning the hood.

45. Forced landing flare - A forced landing flare is carried in a tube fixed inside the fuselage. The flare is released by means of a ring grip on the left of the pilot's seat.

46. First aid - The first aid outfit is stowed aft of the wireless equipment and is accessible through a hinged panel on the port side of the fuselage.

THE OPERATIONAL USE OF 150 GRADE FUEL AND 25 LB. BOOST IN MERLIN 66 ENGINES IN SPITFIRE IX L.F. AIRCRAFT

1. The Portreath wing, consisting of Nos. 1 and 165 Squadrons have been using 150 grade fuel and 25 lbs. boost for the last four weeks on extensive operational flying. Each Squadron has been averaging approximately 35 hours operational flying per day during periods of tine weather.

At the commencement of these trials numerous difficulties were experienced as a result or using the 150 grade fuel, but to a certain extent these are exaggerate by the root that both Squadrons had been re-equipped with brand-new air-craft just prior to the incorporation at the modification, and thus were also experiencing teething troubles.

However, at the and or the period in question, most or the difficulties had been overcome and the use of the 150 grade fuel on operations is now viewed with nothing but extreme satisfaction by all concerned. Reference is made to Headquarters, Air Defence or Great Britain letter ADGB/S. 37041/GTO dated 20th May 1944

2. The type of operations as carried out by this Wing in the last month may be briefly divided into two categories.

Long-range sorties, is which the economical use of fuel becomes a necessity in order to increase endurance and range - i.e. Rangers, Insteps, and 3-hour oversea patrols.

Short-range sorties, where fuel economy is not of primary importance, i.e. Rhubarbs, Rodeos, Roadsteads, and defensive patrols and interceptions.

3. Long Range Sorties - In the early stages it was found by using economical cruising conditions, i.e. 2,000 R.P.M. and 4 lbs. boost, serious leading up or the' plugs resulted despite the tact that the engines were being opened up approximately every half -hour. This began to constitute a serious menace to the success of operations undertaken. Therefore it was decided that as far as possible, extreme economical cruising conditions should not be used as they resulted in the eventual rough running and possible failure or the engine. Furthermore, after such a sortie - when an attempt to use 25 lbs. boost was made the engine showed extreme disinclination to run at this setting, in the form or severe rough running and blow backs at anything from + 12 lbs. to + 25 lbs. boost. Thus by using a setting of 2400 R.P.M. and + 4 lbs. boost and also opening up to 2850 R.P.M. + 12 lbs. for half a minute every 15 minutes, it was found that leading up of the plugs was avoided and that the engine would run most efficiently at + 25 lbs. boost whenever it was required.

The average consumption of fuel it was found increased from approximately 47.14 gallons per hour to 53.5 gallons per hour.

Tactically, the high cruising speed was found to be an advantage except when undertaking escort work in which the bombers were cruising at speeds below 220 M.P.H. A.S. I. However, by the use at turnabouts, and by means or weaving across the bombers track, low duty running conditions of the engine were avoided and close contact was still maintained with the bombers.

4. Short Range Sorties - In general it was found that very few problems arose from short-range sorties. Any engine troubles could be traced back to a long-range sortie where economical cruising conditions had been used. By using 21.00 R.P.M. and a higher boost within the cruising range, as the type of operation would permit, no trouble was experienced. However, as a precaution the engines are now opened up to 2850 R.P.M. and + 12 lbs. boost half a minute every 15 minutes as mentioned in Para. 3 above. On such short range sorties the aircraft and engine are at their best when being used on a high-speed interception, when a high boost and revs are being used continuously. The impression formed in this way is that under such conditions, the Spitfire IX L.F. using 150 grade fuel is the most formidable fighter of its kind now in operation.

Spitfire fighter banking in the clouds.

- C H A P T E R   9 -
HURRICANE OR SPITFIRE DEBATE?

W HICH IS the better Battle of Britain fighter, the Supermarine Spitfire or the Hawker Hurricane? It is a perennial question, which has been debated among pilots, historians and enthusiasts since 1940, and it is a question to which there is no definitive answer. Each aircraft had its strong and weak points and each of us probably has our own favourite – I know I do. The question needs a context. Best at what? Against what?

At the time of the Battle of Britain, the British fighter pilots had no doubts whatsoever about their ability to take on the *Luftwaffe* bombers, which their Hurricanes and Spitfires could out-perform in every department. That said, RAF fighters were brought down and pilots were killed by return fire from the German bombers, so it was still a dangerous occupation.

The *Luftwaffe* single-engine fighter that the RAF pilots faced, the Messerschmitt

Bf 109, was a different proposition though; it was a much more dangerous opponent. Indeed, the Bf 109 accounted for most of the losses suffered by Fighter Command during the Battle. So the real context of the question is, which of the two RAF fighters compared most favourably with the Bf 109, as well as which was 'the best' in terms of the overall victory in the Battle.

The first thing to note is that the RAF fighter pilots at the time of the Battle of Britain did not have any choice over whether they flew Hurricanes or Spitfires. Military organisations are not democracies and the pilots had to go where they were sent and fly what they were told to fly. The RAF fighter pilots of 1940 were undoubtedly proud to fly either type. Both aircraft were considered as modern pieces of equipment at the time, both were pushing the boundaries of performance beyond anything that humans had experienced before. After all, for most normal people at the time, the fastest thing that they had travelled in was a train!

DESIGN AND CONSTRUCTION

When the Battle of Britain commenced, RAF Fighter Command fielded 30 squadrons equipped with Hurricanes and 19 squadrons with Spitfires. On the evening of 14 September, prior to the defining day of the Battle, there were a total of 533 Hurricanes and 269 Spitfires serviceable and available to fight – almost twice as many Hurricanes as Spitfires. So it was twice as likely that a Battle of Britain fighter pilot would go into combat in a Hurricane rather than a Spitfire.

From a strategic point of view, therefore, the Hurricane wins the contest simply because there were almost twice as many of them available to fight during the Battle and it, therefore, played the greater part.

This was no mere accident. Neither was it due only to the fact that the Hurricane entered squadron service eight months ahead of the Spitfire. Sir Sydney Camm's design for the Hurricane followed that of the earlier Hawker biplanes but without the top wing. The rear fuselage from the pilot's seat rearwards was built as a framework of metal longerons, struts and tie-rods with wooden formers and stringers, covered in doped fabric (Irish linen). Designed to use as many as possible of the jigs, tools and skills available at Hawkers, it was a halfway house between the old biplanes and the newer stressed skin designs of the Spitfire and the German Bf 109.

Hawker's use of the old technology ensured that as many Hurricanes as possible could be built rapidly for the war effort. The Air Ministry calculated that building a Spitfire took 15,200 man-hours but a Hurricane took only 10,300. There were other advantages to the construction of the Hurricane. Exploding cannon shells that did terrible damage to metal skin had less effect upon the

Hurricane's tubular metal framework and fabric skin. In addition, early on in the war, the RAF had very few men who understood the complexities of stressed metal construction, but its airframe fitters had spent their lives servicing and rigging aircraft built like the Hurricane and so could keep them serviceable and flying more easily. Many seriously damaged Hurricanes were repaired in squadron workshops while heavily damaged Spitfires were often pulled out of the front line and sent away to maintenance units for repair or were simply written-off.

From the point of view of the pilot in the cockpit, trying to shoot down enemy aircraft while also staying alive, there are several factors which may make one fighter aircraft better than another; among these are: aircraft performance, the visibility from the cockpit, the armament and ease with which the guns could be brought to bear, and survivability.

POWER AND WEIGHT

Engine power and the aircraft's power-to-weight ratio are obvious factors that will affect performance. The Hurricane Mk.I and Spitfire Mk.Ia in service at the time of the Battle of Britain shared the same Rolls-Royce Merlin III engine, driving a three-bladed constant-speed propeller and producing the same amount of power (a nominal 1030hp). Their main opponent, the Bf 109, was fitted with a Daimler-Benz engine, which produced a roughly comparable 1150hp. The Hurricane was the heaviest of the three aircraft (the Bf 109 being the lightest) so it had the worst power to weight ratio. This, coupled with the fact that its airframe and thick wing section produced considerably more aerodynamic drag than either the Spitfire or Bf 109, meant that the Hurricane had the least impressive climb and speed performance figures. The Bf 109 possessed the best power-to-weight ratio of all three fighters and this was reflected in aspects of its impressive 'top-end' performance.

RATE OF CLIMB

Climb rate was an aspect that particularly concerned the RAF fighter pilots during the Battle of Britain. The Hurricanes and Spitfires were almost invariably scrambled to intercept incoming raids, often later than the pilots would have wished. The time taken to climb to height therefore became tactically critical if the RAF pilots were to stand any chance of engaging the enemy formations with an altitude advantage, which in fact they rarely achieved. The Spitfire had a clear performance benefit over the Hurricane in its time to height, taking a minute less to reach 20,000ft. The Bf 109 had a rate of climb superior to both the RAF fighters but this was less of a factor to the Germans during the Battle of Britain as they had plenty of time and distance to achieve their desired height before they were engaged. The Bf 109's excellent climb rate could, however, be used to good effect by experienced *Luftwaffe* pilots during combats, especially if they started off with a height and, therefore, an energy advantage so that diving attacks could be followed by a zoom climb.

Incidentally, the Spitfire's climb rate advantage over the Hurricane was apparent with the BBMF aircraft that I flew. On air tests, a timed climb to 7000ft was conducted and I would expect the Spitfire to be one minute quicker in the climb than the Hurricane.

SPEED

The Hurricane also lost out to the Spitfire and to the Bf 109 in terms of maximum level speed by some margin. Due to the extra drag created by its airframe and thick wing section, and its slightly inferior power-to-weight ratio, the Hurricane could typically manage about 325mph in level flight, some 25mph below the maximum level speed for the Spitfire and the Bf 109. This could be significant, as it could seriously compromise the Hurricane's ability to close on a fast-moving opponent or, perhaps even more important, to get away from one.

ROLL RATE

Many of the Battle of Britain dogfights between Bf 109s and the British fighters started with the 109s bouncing the RAF fighters from above. As long as the RAF fighter pilots saw them coming – and that is a big 'if' – they could roll into a 90 degree banked break-turn and pull hard into the enemy attack. This would almost invariably cause an overshoot by the Bf 109, the pilot of which would be unable to turn with either a Spitfire or a Hurricane. The ability to roll rapidly into such a break turn was therefore vital and the Spitfire had a roll rate advantage over the Hurricane

Spitfire PR Mark XI reconnaissance aircraft of No. 541 Squadron RAF based at Benson, Oxfordshire, England, UK in flight, Jul 1944; note split-pair camera ports under fuselage.

(which was further improved when metal ailerons were fitted to the Spitfire), although the Bf 109 rolled quicker than either of them. All three types suffered from reduced roll rates at high speed when the ailerons became very heavy, but the Spitfire with metal ailerons suffered less from this than the other two types.

TURNING

Once into the break turn, the comparative rates and radii of turn became the important factors. The wing loadings of the Hurricane and Spitfire were almost identical. The Bf 109's was considerably higher. Wing loading is an important factor in how much lift the wing can produce and therefore how much of that can be translated into a turning vector in a steeply banked turn (the lower the wing loading, the better). The Hurricane actually possessed an advantage over the Spitfire in its turning ability, with a fractionally greater turn rate (in degrees per second) and a significantly lower turn radius once the turn had become established and sustained. Both the Spitfire and the Hurricane had a better turn rate and smaller turn radius than the Bf 109 and if well flown, could fare very well in a dogfight with the German fighter. The Hurricane, though, would tend to bleed energy in a hard turn more easily than the Spitfire. This resulted from the lower power-to-weight ratio of the Hurricane compared with the Spitfire and from the higher lift-induced drag that the Hurricane wing produced.

These factors were apparent to me when I flew the BBMF display sequence in both types. With the same power set, the Hurricane would be more inclined to lose speed ('energy') if it was hauled around the sky too tightly, while the Spitfire retained speed in the same manoeuvres. In a prolonged turning combat, the Hurricane pilot would therefore be more likely to find himself relying on his minimum radius of turn rather than having sufficient energy to achieve a higher rate of turn. This would make the Hurricane pilot more defensive and less offensively capable.

The superior turning capabilities of the British fighters meant that Bf 109 pilots were best advised not to get into a turning fight with either the Hurricane or the Spitfire. Their best option was to use 'hit and run' tactics, diving down with superior energy, hoping to attack unseen, then if spotted and if an attack was spoiled by the British fighter's break turn, to disengage, zoom back up or continue on down and away with the extra starting speed. Such tactics were very effective in the early stages of the Battle when the German fighters roamed ahead and above their bombers as a fighter sweep. When the German fighter pilots were ordered to provide their bombers with close escort, their tactical freedom was curtailed and they were less able to utilise the strengths of their own aircraft and instead played into the hands of the British. In these regimes there is no clear winner between the Hurricane and the Spitfire.

STABILITY VERSUS AGILITY

The Hurricane's stability is famed and is usually mentioned in commending the aircraft as a steady gun platform. However, stability and agility are effective opposites in terms of aircraft design and handling. The Hurricane was, indeed is, if my personal experience is anything to go by, a very stable aircraft. If the pilot does not make any control inputs to alter the status quo, the Hurricane is as steady as a rock. However, if the Hurricane pilot wants to manoeuvre his aircraft rapidly in a dynamic environment such as aerial combat, this takes more doing. With the two examples of the Hurricane that I was privileged to fly, which I can only assume are typical, I found that it took a large control input to get the aircraft moving, especially in pitch – a small movement of the control column from the neutral point wouldn't budge it, almost as if there was something of a dead area. Then having got it moving, it was necessary to back off the input so as not to overdo it. I always found this slightly strange compared with all the other aircraft I had flown. In addition, the controls could hardly be called 'well harmonised' as they were weighted differently in roll and pitch.

The Spitfire, on the other hand, is neutrally stable about all axes, the control forces are light even at high speeds (excepting the limitations of the early fabric-covered ailerons on roll control at high speeds), the controls are sensitive and well harmonised and the aircraft is extremely responsive. The Spitfire will maintain a flying attitude with hands and feet off but the pilot can move it quickly and effortlessly into any manoeuvre he desires. This is what makes the Spitfire such a delight to fly – virtual finger-tip control throughout the flight regime – and the reason why anyone who has flown one loves the feel of it and everyone who has read about it wants to experience it.

These differences in the control responses between the Hurricane and the Spitfire will in truth have little bearing on either aircraft's ability or performance in combat, but the Spitfire pilot may well feel more in control of his mount and better able to manoeuvre rapidly, which is a nice feeling. To counter that though, I have had some wartime veteran pilots tell me that they felt they were too 'ham-fisted' for the Spitfire and actually preferred the feeling that the Hurricane needed to be 'hauled around the sky'. I think they were being over-modest as, if anything, the Hurricane is actually more difficult to fly well than the Spitfire.

STALLING

The stalling characteristics of the Hurricane and the Spitfire differ markedly and this could affect the confidence that pilots had in flying their aircraft to the limits and, therefore, in generating the maximum possible turning performance. The Spitfire's beautiful elliptical wingtips are as near to an optimum aerodynamic design as you can get for the speed regime in which it operated. The elliptical wing shape generates the least lift-induced drag by minimising the wing tip vortices. This is one of the principal reasons why the

Spitfire generates less drag than the Hurricane when turning hard. Also, when the wing roots of the Spitfire have stalled, the wingtips will still be flying quite happily, and the ailerons provide good roll control even at the stall.

A stall in the Spitfire is characterised by some buffet being transmitted though the control column from the elevators, giving ample warning, then at the stall a loss of lift and a 'mushing' sensation in a turn, but with no tendency to drop a wing or to flick. The stall in a Spitfire, even in a hard turn, is completely benign and the aircraft can easily be flown to its limit and at its optimum angle of attack with great confidence. In the air the Spitfire was, and is, totally forgiving of any over-enthusiasm by the pilot. The Hurricane on the other hand gives its pilot less warning of the approaching stall and will invariably drop a wing if fully stalled. In a hard turn this might lead to the Hurricane 'flicking' if pulled too hard into the turn. The Spitfire is much the nicer of the two aircraft in this respect.

COCKPIT VISIBILITY

The visibility from the cockpit is obviously of great importance to the fighter pilot if he is to stand any chance of seeing enemy fighters attempting to 'bounce' him before they kill him. The pilot's view from the Spitfire, and again I speak with the privileged benefit of personal experience, is excellent to the side and rear. The 'blown' bubble-shaped canopy-hood allows the Spitfire pilot to see right round behind the aircraft; with the seat harness shoulder straps loosened slightly (the way I always flew, except for take-off or landing) it is possible to twist around so that you can actually see the fin and, more importantly, any other aircraft coming from that direction. The view through the Hurricane's 'lattice-work' canopy is naturally more restricted, and the view to the rear is nowhere near as good as the Spitfire, as the flat sides of the hood stop the pilot from getting his head far enough over and around.

In both aircraft, I personally found the rear-view mirrors to be of limited value, as an attacking aircraft would still be a speck in the mirror when it was at open-fire range – better than nothing though. The one area where the Hurricane has a slight advantage in terms of visibility is over the nose. The Hurricane's slightly sloping nose gives a better view ahead than that over the long straight nose of the Spitfire; and this would allow a Hurricane pilot to pull more lead when taking a deflection shot without losing the intended target under the nose. The Bf 109 pilot, also looking through a 'lattice-work' canopy, had similar problems to the Hurricane pilot.

ARMAMENT AND GUNNERY

During the Battle of Britain, the Hurricane and the Spitfire shared identical armament in the form of eight 0.303 Browning machine guns. (The initially unsuccessful experiments with 20mm cannons on the Spitfire were not to benefit the RAF fighter pilots until after the Battle). The pilots of both RAF fighters had a similar amount of firing time (16 seconds in a Spitfire, 17 seconds in a Hurricane). The Bf 109E was equipped with cannons as well as machine guns and this armament could make its firepower quite devastating against the British fighters. The weight of fire from a three-second burst of gunfire from the Hurricane or Spitfire was 10lb, while for the Bf 109, with cannons and machine guns, it was 18lb.

Every pilot who flew the Hurricane said it was an excellent gun platform, not least because of its rock-steady aircraft stability. In addition, the Hurricane's sturdy wings provided solid bracing for the guns which were mounted in twin batteries of four, closely grouped together in each wing, as close in to the fuselage as they could be placed to clear the propeller. Because of its thin wing, the Spitfire's armament of machine guns had to be spread out along the wing, with the outboard gun a third of the way in from the wingtip, then a group of two and then an inboard gun on each side. The wings would flex in turbulence or when pulling G and so the

Spitfires banking in flight.

guns could be slightly out of line from their ground harmonisation when they were fired, making them less accurate especially over range. Although there is no difference in the armament between the Battle of Britain Hurricanes and Spitfires, the Hurricane was clearly the better gun platform.

SURVIVABILITY

Armour plating provided the pilots of all three types of aircraft with similar levels of protection (by the time of the Battle of Britain). The Hurricane, with its rugged construction, could absorb an enormous amount of punishment and still get the pilot home safely. This was not so true of the rather more delicate Spitfire.

All three of the single-engine fighters, from both sides, suffered from weak or critical points which if hit by enemy gunfire, would bring powered flight to a rapid and premature end. Principal among these were the radiators and cooling systems, which were easily damaged and without which the liquid-cooled engines would not run for long. Of most concern to the pilots was the possibility of fire and, as we know, many of them were terribly burned before they could get out of their cockpits. The fuel tanks in the Spitfire were in the nose, ahead of the pilot and behind the engine. The Hurricane had a fuel tank in each wing and the so-called 'Reserve' fuel tank (rather a misnomer) in the nose ahead of the pilot and above his feet on the rudder pedals. These fuel tanks were supposedly 'self sealing', but this system did not work against cannon shells which would cause too great a rupture and an almost immediate fire, which could easily spread into the cockpit, especially in the case of the Hurricane.

When the pilots opened the cockpit canopy to bale out, this drew the flames further into the cockpit like a blowtorch. Neither the Spitfire nor the Hurricane was immune from this possibility and there was not much to choose between them in these terms, although the positioning of the Hurricane's tank above the pilot's feet was perhaps the least desirable. There is no indication that baling out of either aircraft was more difficult, or less likely to be successful, than the other.

One important aspect of survivability was landing! The Hurricane had a distinct advantage over both the Spitfire and the Bf 109 because of the relative ease with which it could be landed. The view over the nose of the Hurricane makes it easier to see ahead on the approach to land. The wide, sturdy undercarriage (coupled with effective rudder control when the tail is down) gives much better directional stability and control on the ground. The Hurricane was far better suited to rough landing strips and landings in less than ideal circumstances. With the Spitfire, on the other hand, the narrow-track undercarriage does not assist the aircraft to 'tramline' on the ground, and the relatively small fin and rudder do not endow it with great directional control, especially once the tail wheel is down on the ground and the nose and fuselage are blanking the tail. Where the Spitfire is forgiving of its pilot in the air, the Hurricane is the more forgiving of any mistakes by its pilot on landing. (The Bf 109 rightly had a notorious reputation for landing accidents and some 10 per cent of the losses of Bf 109s occurred on landing.)

HURRICANE OR SPITFIRE?

The question of which is the best Battle of Britain fighter – Hurricane or Spitfire – does not have a definitive answer. Each aircraft had its advantages and its disadvantages. Each was created under a completely different set of circumstances and came from totally different backgrounds and antecedents; they could not, in fact, have been more different from one another. What is clear is that, within the context of the Battle of Britain, and using the 'yardstick' of the Bf 109 as the most capable opponent they had to face, the advantages and disadvantages of each were not particularly significant and tended to balance each other out. Both aircraft were equally capable fighters in the combat environment they faced during the Battle, and they both played a decisive and equally vital role in the eventual victory.

Statistics from modern research show that the 19 Spitfire squadrons operating during the Battle of Britain are credited with 521 victories (an average of just over 27 per squadron) and a victory-to-loss ratio of 1.8:1. In comparison, the 30 fully engaged Hurricane squadrons are credited with 655 victories (an average of just fewer than 22 per squadron) and victory-to-loss ratio of 1.34:1. On the basis of the statistics alone, therefore, perhaps the Spitfire has a slight edge. We know that it was the Spitfire that the German Bf 109 fighter pilots feared the most; they felt that they should not fall victim to a Hurricane's guns, although, of course, many did.

From a purely personal point of view, if my time as an RAF fighter pilot had started during the Battle of Britain, I would, I am sure, have felt quite confident going into combat in a Hurricane. That said, with the benefit of the experience of flying both, I would choose the Spitfire if I had the choice. As one Battle of Britain veteran said to me when I asked him the question a few years ago: "The Hurricane was all right until you flew a Spitfire!" There were, however, a number of fighter pilots during the Battle who flew Spitfires first and then transitioned on promotion to Hurricanes, invariably without complaint.

CONCLUSION

More telling than attempting to differentiate between the advantages and disadvantages of the Hurricane and the Spitfire is the conclusion that the RAF fighter pilots did not have vastly superior equipment to the opposition during the Battle of Britain. I have suggested that there are three tangibles that could affect the outcome of aerial combat: superior equipment, tactics and training/experience. Not only was there not a significant advantage in equipment, but also neither was there in the other two factors. British tactics were poor when the Battle began although they steadily improved. The initial tight formations flown by Fighter Command, with elements of three aircraft in a 'Vic', were a hangover from peacetime training and meant that most of the pilots in the formation were concentrating on station-keeping rather than looking out to avoid being bounced.

The Germans, meanwhile, started well with their more flexible and manoeuvrable tactical formations and by working to the strengths of their Bf 109s by sweeping ahead and above the bombers. They lost their tactical advantage when they were tied to providing close escorts to the bombers.

The pilots on both sides were trained to similar standards. Even those young RAF fighter pilots who were famously thrown into battle with very few flying hours on Spitfires or Hurricanes had typically received over 150 hours of previous flying training of a high standard. The RAF fighter pilots were in many cases short of combat experience compared with the *Luftwaffe* pilots, but if they lived through the first few fights, this was quickly rectified.

So, if there was no particular advantage to the RAF pilots over the Germans in equipment, tactics or training/experience, how did victory in the Battle of Britain come the way of the British? It leaves only the conclusion that the real key to the victory lay in the RAF pilots themselves. Their character and determination, their aggression, courage and sheer fighting spirit, aspects which I earlier suggested ought perhaps not to be relied upon for guaranteed victory, were in fact the deciding factor. It really was a close run thing!

CHAPTER 10

VN496 : THE LAST SPITFIRE

O N THE 20th February 1948, almost twelve years from the prototype's first flight, the last production Spitfire, an F Mk 24 (VN496) left the production line. Some 22,759 Spitfire's and Seafire's were built over a 10 year production run during which time Reginald Mitchell's classic design evolved almost beyond recognition into 24 different marks.

The Spitfire was the worlds only fighter aircraft in series production before, during, and after the Second World War, and served with many of the world's airforces well into the 1960's!

MORE FROM THE SAME SERIES

Most books from the 'World War II from Original Sources' series are edited and endorsed by Emmy Award winning film maker and military historian Bob Carruthers, producer of Discovery Channel's Line of Fire and Weapons of War and BBC's Both Sides of the Line. Long experience and strong editorial control gives the military history enthusiast the ability to buy with confidence.

The series advisor is David McWhinnie, producer of the acclaimed Battlefield series for Discovery Channel. David and Bob have co-produced books and films with a wide variety of the UK's leading historians including Professor John Erickson and Dr David Chandler.

Where possible the books draw on rare primary sources to give the military enthusiast new insights into a fascinating subject.

For more information visit www.pen-and-sword.co.uk